LOST
HANCOCK
COUNTY
OHIO

LOST
HANCOCK
COUNTY
OHIO

TERESA STRALEY LAMBERT

THE
History
PRESS

Published by The History Press
Charleston, SC
www.historypress.net

Front cover: Kirk Milling survived many Findlay floods over the years. *Courtesy of the Hancock Historical Museum.*

Back cover: An employee works at the Kirk Milling Company during the 1930s. *Courtesy of the Hancock Historical Museum.*

First published 2019

Manufactured in the United States

ISBN 9781467141352

Library of Congress Control Number: 2019944012

Dedicated to my family, my friends, and the people of Hancock County, Ohio.

CONTENTS

CONTENTS

ACKNOWLEDGEMENTS

I had no idea when embarking on this journey that I would be so totally immersed in the history of Findlay and Hancock County, Ohio. Although I have lived in Findlay for more than forty years, it was not until I began volunteering at the Hancock Historical Museum after retiring from a teaching career that I discovered countless fascinating places that I had never heard of right here in Findlay and the surrounding county. As I read and researched and gave museum tours to youngsters and presented historical programs to those in retirement communities and senior centers, I knew that a "Lost Hancock County" book would be a perfect avenue for sharing some of this newfound—yet old—information.

Many people have helped and encouraged me in this endeavor. The staff at the Hancock Historical Museum helped in countless ways. Executive director Sarah Sisser offered ideas and sources. Curator/archivist Joy Bennet was an invaluable help in finding, scanning and sharing photographs. So many sources, so little time! Friend and colleague Deb Wickerham, the museum's education coordinator, also provided much-appreciated information. Laurel Etler, special events and communications coordinator, always greeted me with a warm, friendly smile, even when I needed to get into the museum during "closed" hours.

Thanks to *Courier* writer Jeanne Wiley Wolf, who shared many ideas and sources.

Spending time at the Findlay–Hancock County Public Library and its branch in McComb put me in touch with knowledgeable staff, useful books and archival newspapers.

ACKNOWLEDGEMENTS

Interviewing locals of Hancock County enabled me to add a personal touch to many of the stories. Thanks to E. Tom Child, Sue Child, Dave Davis, Ann DeWitt, Deb Ewing, Ginny Motter, Barbara Myers, Bill Phillips, Jack Ridge, Barbara von Stein Smith, Doug Smith, Don Steinman, Joe Wasson and Phyllis Benton Wiegand for sharing your time and stories.

My editor at The History Press, John Rodrigue, was with me from the start, allowing me to work at my own pace, always reassuring me that I was on the right track.

As a member of the Literal Women Book Club for over thirty-five years, I must thank this sisterhood for its enduring support: Cindy Benton, Sharon Brubeck, Chris Fox, Judy Hall, Charlene Hankinson, Trish McClosky, Kathy Qualkenbush and Vicki Sherman.

Last but not least, my family. My son, Scott, suggested invaluable ideas and editorial advice; my daughter, Kate, and her history-teacher husband, Jon, provided more moral support than anyone should have to, not to mention buoying me up with visits from grandsons Otto and Frank, named for family ancestors; and my husband, Randy, who only interrupted my writing hundreds (maybe thousands) of times just to see if I wanted more coffee or a snack. He supported me throughout this journey while patiently waiting for our next adventure. Thank you, my dears, one and all.

INTRODUCTION

Although Hancock County, Ohio, covers around 530 square miles of land, less than 2 percent of that area is comprised of urban districts. Today, more than a dozen towns exist, but several more have faded away. The county itself is made up of seventeen townships named for explorers, military men, political people and settlers. Hancock County towns and villages continue to adapt to the changes that have occurred over the past two hundred years.

The county has always been an agricultural region and remains so today. Early pioneers of the 1820s and 1830s cleared the land, built cabins and created farms and towns. Related pursuits led to the creation of mills, dairies and hatcheries. Corn, wheat, oats and soybeans were introduced early in the county's history and are still being produced there but with modern, more efficient equipment.

In the mid-1880s, gas and oil were discovered in Hancock County; this boosted the economies of many towns, especially the county seat of Findlay, and the population of Findlay and surrounding towns ballooned so much that many people predicted that Toledo would soon be a suburb of Findlay! They also predicted that the gas and oil would last forever. They were wrong on both counts, but during that short window of time, many factories and businesses flourished. Factories produced the daily essentials—everything from furniture and glassware to underwear and gloves. Other factories created more curious things, such as masks, medicines and cigars.

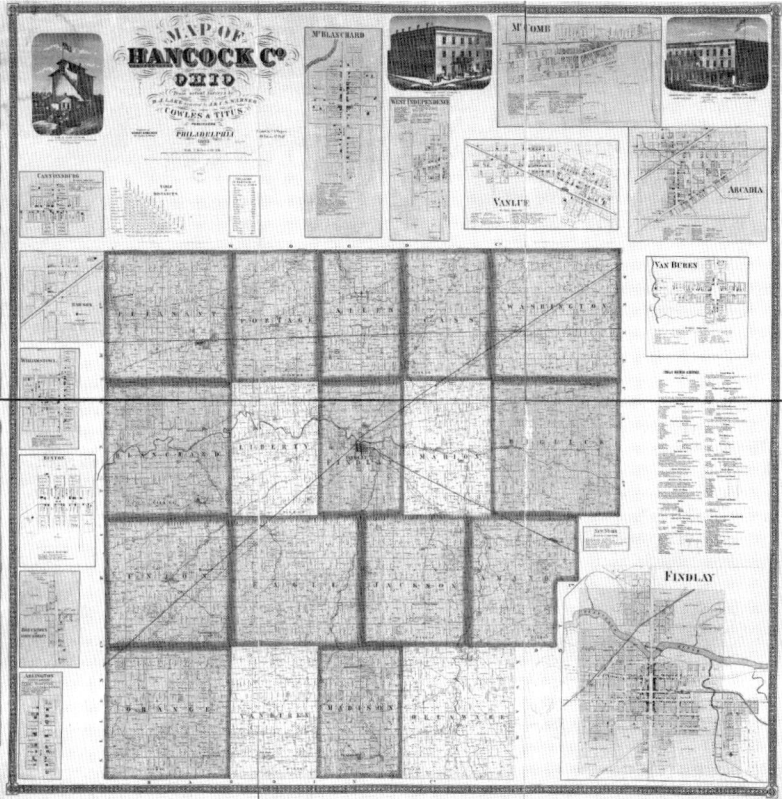

An 1863 map of Hancock County, Ohio, depicts the seventeen townships and many of the towns and villages of the time. *Courtesy of the Hancock Historical Museum.*

Another contributing factor in the growth of these modest towns was the coming of the railroads. Some towns began with high hopes only to be stalled by lack of progress or not being on the projected route after changes had been made. Streetcars and interurban trains allowed people to visit friends and relatives more quickly and easily in the surrounding towns, and cars and trucks were actually being manufactured in Findlay.

In this new era of mechanical transportation, not only was it easier to visit other places, but people could also travel more easily to entertainment venues, such as opera houses, theaters and parks. These locations provided great entertainment, including vaudeville shows, revues, lectures, plays, concerts and "moving pictures."

But, as they say, nothing lasts forever. Although many of the area's buildings remain standing and are being used in other capacities, their original purposes have been lost to generations. Other buildings are simply no longer there due to flooding, fires or the need for parking lots. Many readers may have memories of some of the "lost" places in this book; others may be surprised at what used to be in Hancock County.

PART 1: THE CREAM AND THE CROPS—AGRICULTURE

1

RUN OF THE MILL

The popular tune of 1910, "Down by the Old Millstream," was written by Hancock County, Ohio native son Tell Taylor, a vaudevillian who was born on a farm near Vanlue. According to legend, Taylor grew up swimming and fishing in the Blanchard River and held fond memories of the Misamore Mill in Amanda Township.

Although this early gristmill and the bridge near it no longer exist, Taylor's lyrics retain the perception of the romance of the river and the values of the early settlers of the county and their tenacity in creating mills.

EARLY MILLS—HANCOCK COUNTY

The Great Black Swamp. Dense forests. Wild animals. Wyandot, Shawnee, Delaware and Ottawa tribes. The Blanchard River. One "real" road—a military trail created during the War of 1812. These were the elements of the area that became Hancock County when settlers began arriving in northwest Ohio.

As Hancock County was being established in the 1820s and 1830s, settlers knew the hardships of clearing the land, felling trees to build cabins and establishing small farms for their subsistence. They tended to put down roots near the Blanchard River and its many tributaries, allowing for the creation of water-powered mills, although some mills relied on steam power,

Tell Taylor, a Hancock County native famous for composing the song "Down by the Old Millstream," is honored with this memorial at Riverside Park in Findlay. *Courtesy of the author.*

horsepower or even manpower. Eventually, gristmills and flouring mills, lumber mills, sawmills, planing mills, hoop mills, stave mills, barrel mills and woolen, flax and linseed mills could be found in almost every township in the county. All were necessary for area residents to grind grains for their own food and to feed their livestock, cut seasoned lumber in order to build cabins and furniture, create containers for holding whatever needed to be held and weave textiles to turn them into clothing and household items. From Hancock County's early beginnings and throughout the nineteenth and early twentieth centuries, mills have held a place of great importance in its history.

Even though most settlers established small farms and communities along the Blanchard River, it was quite some time before any mills were created to grind their corn or wheat. The pioneers, both men and women, would have to grind corn or pound wheat by hand if they wanted cornpone or flour pastries. Even after some mills were finally built, they were sometimes so distant that it would take days for a farmer to travel the rugged terrain in order to be able to provide grains for his family.

One of the first mills in the county was a hand mill built by Godfrey Wolford in 1826 in Delaware Township near the village of Mt. Blanchard. Pioneers had to travel many miles to get to this mill, but as Robert C. Brown explained in his *History of Hancock County*:

> *Mr. Wolford was a blacksmith and therefore a very useful man. For the convenience of the settlers he set up the mill in the open space between the double log-cabin of Ephraim Elder, where each man did his own grinding, and no charges were made. This rude mill served the purpose till 1829–1830, when Mr. Wolford erected a grist-mill on the Blanchard in Section 11, which was the first flouring-mill operated in the county outside of Findlay.*

Wolford replacing his hand mill with a gristmill illustrates the evolution of some mills. This eased the problem of the settlers' ability to procure grains for making breads. Wolford's mill was successful; it was assessed several years later at $500 (over $14,000 in today's money). Although the production of this mill was influenced by freezing temperatures in winter and dry spells in the summer, Wolford was able to keep enough flour in stock to help the settlers during these downtimes. He later sold the gristmill to John Hanley, who added a sawmill. A new owner, George Silas Fahl (pronounced Fail), continued these mills and, along with his son Silas, operated them well into the late nineteenth century. According to Brown:

> *In 1862 our subject came into possession of the mill which was established by Godfrey Wolford, and now operates as a grist and flouring-mill with a saw-mill addition. In 1872 he established a steam planing-mill, shingle-mill, lath factory, etc., to which he added, in 1880, the cider-mill which took the premium at the Centennial Exposition in Philadelphia, Penn, and he makes over 75,000 gallons of cider per year. Mr. Fahl is an energetic business man, highly respected by the entire community.*

The Misamore Mill was located in Amanda Township along the Blanchard River. Michael Misamore settled in Hancock County in the early 1830s, constructing his mill in 1835. It was not only the first mill in that township but also the first frame building to be erected there. This water-powered mill was also adversely affected by fluctuating seasonal temperatures. However, it continued to be used by the Misamore family and subsequent owners into the late nineteenth century.

Another early water-powered mill built by John Burman in Allen Township did not last long due to the unreliability of the water level in the creek east of the community of Van Buren. In fact, people had to travel from Van Buren to Findlay, Perrysburg or Sandusky for their flour and meal—distances of seven, thirty-one and sixty-two miles away, respectively. In 1859, a mill in the Van Buren area began to handle grist brought there from Bowling Green and the surrounding region and eventually added a sawmill.

More Mills—Hancock County

Later in the nineteenth century, the arrival of the railroad aided in promoting business in some of the outlying areas of the county. For example, in Cory (today's Mt. Cory), Cory's Flouring Mill and Grist Mill were built in 1873 by Dr. H.P. Eaten. In 1877, Levi Falk bought this mill and successfully operated it until fire destroyed it in 1895. Falk, having come to Mt. Cory at the age of one in 1848, became a successful businessman in the village. In *A Centennial Biographical History of Hancock County, Ohio (1903)*, he is described as a man who

> *next began making extensive deals in hay, shipping it to various points, but in 1902 he discontinued his active business career, and while he is too young and vigorous to go on the retired list, he takes life more leisurely and does not find it necessary to push forward with the energy he has displayed in the past.*

That is, if you call managing a 160-acre farm "leisurely."

Vanlue, in Amanda Township, was another community that benefited from the railroad, as it was on the branch between Findlay and Carey. A gristmill built in 1855 by Hiram Russell became the Centennial Mills of the 1880s. Vanlue's location on the railroad made it an important point for shipping goods to other parts of the county.

Several kinds of mills were located in the village of Benton Ridge in Blanchard Township. One, a sawmill, began in the 1860s and provided much of the lumber for the buildings of the town. It ran until it closed in 1904. Another lumber mill was in business from the late 1800s until around 1919. A grist/flour mill operated from the late 1800s until it closed in 1906. The buildings remained until the early 1920s, when they were demolished.

In 1885, the leasing of a lot for the creation of the Jenera Roller Mills came with a stiff set of rules. The lessees had to agree to the following:

The mill is to be kept in good running order and that the premises shall be used and occupied in a careful, safe and proper manner. All fires therein are to be kept, shall be safely secured, kept, and conducted – nor shall liquor, whether Spiritus, Venous or Fermented be sold either at wholesale or retail on premises without consent in writing under pain of forfeiting.

WATERLOO MILL—WATERLOO (NEAR ARLINGTON)

During the War of 1812, General William Hull traveled with troops through western Ohio to Detroit, with the final goal being to secure Detroit and attack Canada. The trek from Urbana, Ohio, to Detroit required Hull and his 1,500 or so men to traverse the Great Black Swamp of northwestern Ohio, creating "Hull's Trace." Hull's Trace verged the west side of Eagle Creek in Hancock County. As local historian Don Steinman wrote in the ECHO (Eagle Creek Historical Organization) newsletter, "It should be noted that local legend has it that travel was so muddy and rugged in the heavily forested Waterloo area, that they actually buried several canons [*sic*] in that vicinity. Get those metal detectors out!"

Many soldiers stationed at Fort Findlay chose to settle in the area following the war, as did pioneers traveling to northwest Ohio. Hull's Road eventually became U.S. Route 68, a thoroughfare from Springfield to Findlay, and many towns, villages and hamlets sprang up near it.

One such community was Waterloo, a small settlement not far from today's Arlington, which began when one of Hull's soldiers, Simeon Ransbottom, decided to build a cabin there in 1825. Between 1826 and 1835, several families came to call Waterloo home. John and Caroline Diller, who bought Ransbottom's land when he moved on, operated a hotel/tavern named Cross Keys. It was the first hotel or tavern in Madison Township and was located on the west bank of Eagle Creek at Waterloo.

"There are two theories on how Waterloo got its name," writes Steinman. "One was because of the water from Eagle Creek being there. The other is that many a man met his Waterloo (just as Napoleon did), drinking whiskey at the Cross Keys Tavern."

D.B. Beardsley describes the people of Waterloo in perhaps a more positive light in his 1881 *History of Hancock County*:

> *The people of this township devote themselves to agricultural pursuits, and are a peaceable, quiet and thrifty community. Education and religion command the respect and attention of all. The first settlers are principally from the eastern part of the State and from Pennsylvania. There are, however, quite a number of German, and their descendants.*

By 1838, Martin Funk brought his family to Waterloo and started the first gristmill. At that time, people in the area had to travel many miles to grind their wheat, rye, buckwheat or corn, so they were grateful to finally have a mill so near.

This first mill in Madison Township burned down around 1850. Funk then decided to build a new mill, eliciting the aid of talented woodworker Henry Hull, a German immigrant. The new mill was to be a gristmill and a sawmill. The people of the area were delighted. In fact, they volunteered their time to help construct two millraces. According to the book *The Village of Arlington, 1834–1984*:

> *They did it by hand, using only shovels and wheelbarrows. The race took the water from Eagle Creek above the Funk dwelling. It passed in front of the house, crossing the road after leaving the mill, and emptied into the creek many rods below the mill. The race had two gates, one at the head of the race, another at the mill. A pole with planks attached spanned the race and was lowered when the water was not needed and raised to allow the current to enter the race.*

The Funk Mill had three waterwheels, a perpendicular shaft and a rather primitive saw, but it was successful in that it could not only grind grain but also cut logs on either side of the mill. Oftentimes, during the summer, water slowed in Eagle Creek. Martin Funk's son John would then travel to Hardin County, just south of Hancock County, to try to get a stronger flow of water to come to the mill.

John Funk moved to Michigan after several years of running the mill, selling it to his brother-in-law Nicholas Price. Price ran the mill alone until his sons were old enough to help. The mill consisted of two floors above the power room and was large enough to require a large bell to be rung to gain the miller's attention whether he was on the top or bottom floor.

Strong competition from roller mills in neighboring communities—and the fact that the water supply was running out, and no roads or railroads were near Waterloo—resulted in Nicholas Price closing down the mill, leaving it idle for several years. Price's obituary in the April 6, 1910 *Arlingtonian* recalls his community spirit in several ways: "Repeatedly were people known to come to him having neither money or wheat to offer in exchange for flour and yet were sorely in need of the same but were never known to be turned from his mills empty handed." The Waterloo Mill, aka Funk's Mill and Price's Mill, lasted until around 1882, about the same time that the Cleveland, Delphos & St. Louis Railroad was built through Arlington.

In 1884, after erecting an elevator building on railroad-leased property in Arlington, owner Peter Traucht purchased the contents of the old Waterloo Mill, rebuilding it next to the elevator. He added a roller mill and steam engine but also incorporated some of the old equipment. A buhr (the hard rock used to build millstones) continued to grind corn, rye and buckwheat for meal, flour and feed.

Henry Hull, the German immigrant who helped with the construction of so many mills in Hancock County, including the Fahl Mill near Mt. Blanchard, is also credited with building the first power gristmill in Ohio.

"No man of little courage, patience or inventive genius would ever have attempted the stupendous task of effecting a power wheel 60 feet in diameter, set at the correct incline, all parts wrought by hand, even to the cogs in the wheels," the *Findlay Republican Courier* reported in June 1937. And yet, he did that—and more.

An educated man, Hull had mastered just about every kind of math imaginable while he was a young man in Germany. Thus, he was able to construct things in his mind before constructing them on the land. He created his mill from the timber standing on his farm. Upon completion, the mill served farmers from throughout the county. Men with horse- or oxen-drawn wagons of grain, sometimes ten to fifteen teams, filled the mill yard while waiting their turns at the mill. Since the mill operated from early morning until it was too dark to continue, it was not unusual for some farmers to spend the night while waiting. Many slept in their wagons or on the second floor of the mill.

Shortly after completing the mill for Funk, Henry Hull passed away, but his legacy lived on. His two sons, George and Andrew, became carpenters, as did George's four sons and a grandson.

After his father's death, George Hull enhanced the mill by adding a horse-powered turning lathe to fashion spindles and hubs for spinning wheels. As reported in the *Findlay Republican Courier*:

The large wheels were five feet in diameter for spinning yarn and carded wool. This wheel was run by hand. The operator would give the wheel a spin which would give it sufficient momentum to spin from 30 to 40 feet of yarn. This was then put on a reel, also made by Mr. Hull. This action was repeated until there was enough yarn for a skein.

The ever-innovative George Hull also devised a special gear that snapped when a spring was released, allowing for each skein of yarn to hold exactly the same number of yards. He also developed a flax spinning wheel that was powered by a treadle. Following the Civil War and a short stint in farming, George Hull began manufacturing coffins and often officiated at funerals in the southern part of the county.

Eagle Mills/Kirk Milling—Findlay

In 1845, Martin Huber, John Julien and John Engelman bought a lot on Sandusky Street, just east of Eagle Creek, and built Findlay's first flouring mill. Eagle Mills was one of the first steam-powered mills in Hancock County. Following Martin Huber's death in 1846, his brother Benjamin Huber purchased the mill, operating it until 1865. Fourteen years and many owners later, in 1879, thirty-year-old David Kirk arrived in Findlay and became co-owner of the mills with W.W. McConnell. Kirk purchased McConnell's interest in the mill in 1885. At that time, wrote Robert C.

WE BUY
WHEAT-CORN-OATS
ASK US FOR PRICES BEFORE SELLING

EAGLE MILLS

USE **NEW-PROCESS** OR **SNOW-BALL**
Our "QUALITY" FLOURS

DAVID KIRK   -   -   FINDLAY, OHIO

David Kirk's Eagle Mills advertises its quality flours. Courtesy of the Hancock Historical Museum.

Brown, "The Eagle Mills are now first-class in their appointments, and are averaging 125 barrels of a superior grade of flour every twenty-four hours, though having a capacity of 150 barrels." Brown goes on to describe Kirk as "a hardworking, painstaking and industrious business man, and has, by his own exertions, built up his present extensive business and his large trade is the result of first-class work."

As Findlay was basking in the glow of the gas boom, a March 1887 *Hancock Courier* article reported, "Mr. Kirk, at a cost of $2,000, drilled and equipped his well for running his large flour mill, thereby saving annually a fuel bill of $2,500 and having a surplus enough to run the Findlay woolen mills and supplying a number of private consumers."

A reporter for the *Weekly Jeffersonian* visited Eagle Mills in 1894 and wrote of his observations and experiences during the visit. Noting that improvements in modern machinery had brought great results to the flouring industry in the past ten years, he stated, "We find that the advancement is remarkable." After David Kirk purchased the mill in 1885, he set about refitting it with new machinery and more modern methods, which increased the number of patrons buying flour.

Kirk Milling survived many Findlay floods over the years. *Courtesy of the Hancock Historical Museum.*

The mill itself was a three-story building with a basement and a storage area for feed. "Its capacity is 175 barrels of flour per day," the *Hancock Courier* article continued, "besides a large quantity of mill feed. It consumes 800 bushels of wheat per day, and when running on full time, fourteen persons are employed in the mill." A nearby cooper shop made barrels used for packing the flour.

Three grades of flour were made at this mill: "Kirk's New Process," a "light, sweet wholesome bread" that included more nutritional grades of wheat; "White Loaf," also a fine bread; and "Snow Ball," a straight grade that bakers used.

The major improvement made at this mill included the use of rollers rather than millstones. With the roller process, the wheat was brushed and scoured, thus ridding it of impurities and dust. Different grades went in different directions. The improved machinery resulted in a much purer and more nutritious flour. "It is conceded by competent judges," stated the reporter, "that twenty-two pounds more bread can be made from a barrel of flour made by rolls than by the old system of flour made on mill stones."

An employee works at the Kirk Milling Company during the 1930s. *Courtesy of the Hancock Historical Museum.*

The Kirk Milling Company continued to be active in the 1950s. *Courtesy of the Hancock Historical Museum.*

The article concluded with the assertion that Eagle Mills directly benefited Findlay and Hancock County: "The fact that the flour finds a ready market abroad as well as at home, and is a favorite wherever introduced, is the best evidence of its superior merits."

David Kirk, once described as a "busy worker all his life, having been from boyhood a miller, and a good one," died on December 12, 1922. After his death, Eagle Mills became Kirk Milling Company.

Other types of mills in Findlay included the Findlay Woolen Mills, Findlay Linseed Oil Mill and Findlay Flax Mill. The woolen mill was located in the remodeled Presbyterian church on Crawford Street in Findlay. William Anderson and John D. McKibben had bought the building and in 1858 turned it into the Findlay Woolen Mills. At that time, they had four looms and two hundred spindles. Several years later, in 1865, they sold the building and erected a new three-story brick building on East Main Cross Street, east of Eagle Creek. The cornerstone, said Robert C. Brown, "was laid with imposing ceremonies, as there were thousands of people in town that day celebrating over the fall of Richmond and the surrender of Lee's army." This building doubled the capacity of the first, with eight looms and four hundred

This building is all that remains today of the Kirk Milling Company. *Courtesy of the author.*

THOSE WHO WANT

TO PROCURE

Fall and Winter Goods

Should take into consideration two facts, viz: Cheapness and Durability, and to such we would say that the

Findlay Woolen Mills

Is the place to procure Goods that are

WARRANTED TO GIVE FULL SATISFACTION!

In both particulars. The quality of their

Cassimeres, Satinets, Jeans and Flannels,

Cannot be excelled by any Manufactory in Northwestern Ohio. Give them a call and they will prove to you the truth of this assertion.

WM. ANDERSON & CO.

Sept. 30, 1869–n43tf.

An 1869 advertisement for Findlay Woolen Mills lures buyers with "cheapness and durability." *Courtesy of the Hancock Historical Museum.*

spindles. In addition, it housed an office, sales showroom and dye house. By the mid-1880s, the mill was processing fifty thousand pounds of wool into "cassimeres, satinets, blankets, flannels and yarns." Both cassimere, an archaic form of "cashmere," and satinet are types of fabric made from wool and other fibers.

When Findlay Woolen Mills changed locations in 1865, James Adams, William Anderson and Calvin Croninger bought the old building on Crawford Street, renovating it for use as the Findlay Linseed Oil Mill. Linseed is created by pressing dried flax plant seeds. This mill ran successfully for many years, through many changes in the building and in ownership. During the 1880s, the linseed mill employed six men and had a yearly capacity of forty-five thousand bushels of seed.

Also in 1865, S.F. Gray, J.S. Patterson and Milton Taylor turned an old foundry on East Crawford Street into a flax mill. During the 1880s, the flax mill tried to increase business with newspaper advertisements asking for longer as well as "tramped or rolled" straw and short articles of interest aimed toward area farmers and promoting the virtues of flax as a money crop. This mill did not fare as well as the others, and it eventually became a storage area for baling hay.

MILKING IT FOR ALL IT'S WORTH

What started for many settlers as the necessity of having a milk cow to provide ingredients for milk, cheese, cream and butter grew to Hancock County boasting dozens of dairy farms at one time. Many of the communities in the county eventually had dairies that supplied these essential products to the surrounding areas. From milk being delivered by horse and wagon to the local huckster service of picking up milk and cream from farmers to take into town and distributing other foodstuffs on the return trip from town to the farms, dairies were an important part of life.

But just like the glass bottles of milk delivered to one's doorstep, many dairies ceased to exist before the end of the twentieth century.

MT. BLANCHARD DAIRIES

All that is left of the Homestead Dairy in Mt. Blanchard is a dilapidated brick house. But in its day, that dairy served an important purpose in Delaware Township. C.B. Hammond operated the Homestead Dairy around 1914–16. He seemed to be a caring, conscientious entrepreneur. A local news item printed in the *Mt. Blanchard Journal* on September 11, 1914, illustrates his honesty:

> *Owing to the extreme high price of good cows and the still higher prices of all feed, dairy supplies, etc., it will be necessary to raise the price of milk to*

meet the increased expenses. On and after October 1, tickets will be sold at the rate of five quarts for 30c, ten for 60c, ten pints for 30c, twenty for 60c and so on. Thanking all our patrons for past favors and hoping to continue in your service, we remain

Yours respectfully,
THE HOMESTEAD DAIRY

The next year, in the *Mt. Blanchard Journal,* Hammond showed his concern for the health and safety of those who purchased his milk and dairy products.

We wish to inform our patrons that we can supply their needs in milk and cream and extra orders will receive our prompt attention. We urge that extra care be taken in cleansing and scalding the bottles now that warm weather is here, also that the bottles be returned promptly and regularly. When no bottle is out and we are not requested to leave milk we will infer that none is wanted. – Homestead Dairy.

After explaining in the September 24, 1915 issue of the *Mt. Blanchard Journal* that the rumors of his dairy's demise had been greatly exaggerated, it was but a mere six months later that he sold his business to Lemuel Sampson, who promised the same morning delivery and prices as Hammond had offered.

In 1917, Sampson, having changed the name of the dairy to Riverside Dairy, had to increase prices for a quart of milk by three cents "to help out a little." That year, he announced:

The Riverside Dairy has installed a milk cooling system and aerator which will add to the keeping qualities of the milk, and as we are through the feeding season of high-priced feed, we will fall back to our old price of 6c per quart. We wish to thank our customers for their patronage, and especially those who stayed by us through the winter. Yours truly, Lemuel Sampson

Emmanuel Leichty, a dairy farmer who lived just east of Mt. Blanchard, delivered milk in a horse-drawn wagon to the people of that community and the surrounding area during the early 1920s. At that time, he charged twelve cents a quart for delivery and ten cents if patrons wished to call for it.

During the late 1920s, Ellsworth D. Powell lived on a farm north of Mt. Blanchard and raised dairy cattle, running a milk delivery service for nine years. In 1933, he decided to retire and sold his equipment to Mt. Blanchard dairy owner R.O. Hellwarth. Powell stated: "Since establishing his dairy on south Main street some two years ago Mr. Hellwarth has enjoyed a liberal patronage and has served his customers in a pleasing manner. He has a modern outfit and is in every way fitted to take care of the combined trade."

Two years later, in 1935, Hellwarth started the Mt. Blanchard Dairy. His local news item printed in the *Mt. Blanchard Journal* in January 1935 illustrates his belief in the business as well as the promise of a prosperous future:

MT. BLANCHARD DAIRY

The Mt. Blanchard Dairy has been set up with the idea of being Permanent in giving service of quality milk on a prompt and regular schedule. It is equipped with an up to date cooling and refrigeration system for the benefit of the folks of Mt. Blanchard. There is no day city service that will excel it. It has been the policy of trying to operate at a price that would be in keeping with the times and the Dairy will practice that in the future. Just recently we have made adjustment in which we can serve you better than before and are endeavoring to give you this service at prices that shall be in keeping with the times as they come along. If better service can be worked out at any time we will be able to do it, and on a permanent basis. It is being desired at this time to give you twice a day delivery, and for your benefit your support is desired. Remember that it takes good feed, good equipment and support from you to insure you a permanent service of good quality milk.

May we count on you?

Yours very truly,
R.O. Hellwarth

Sadly, Hellwarth died of pneumonia on December 31, 1937, at which time Leichty again took over the responsibilities of delivering milk for three years before selling his milk equipment to Harry Lauck. The amazing camaraderie among these dairymen, as well as their common desire to supply the best service to their customers, continued, as displayed in the following notice that appeared in the *Mt. Blanchard Journal* on March 7, 1941, when Leichty turned over the business to Lauck:

These buildings near Mt. Blanchard are the remnants of the Homestead Dairy and Leichty farm. *Courtesy of the author.*

I hope you will continue with Mr. Lauck, for I think he will give you the best of service. I also kindly ask those who have not been patronizing the dairy to do so for Mr. Lauck as he has made a sizeable investment in this business and deserves your patronage. Again I want to thank you one and all for the patronage I so appreciated during my years in the dairy business. E. Leichty

EAST-VIEW JERSEY FARM—FINDLAY

Following in his mailman father's footsteps, Leland King, as a teenager, began his career delivering mail in 1903. He traveled the twenty-six-mile route each day by various means of transportation: walking, bicycling (in the summer) or hitching horses to a cart, mail wagon, buggy or sleigh during the other seasons of the year. According to his granddaughter, Barbara von Stein Smith, Leland stretched the truth about his age by a year in order to get his own route. Born in December 1885, he would have been only seventeen, rather than the "legal" eighteen, when he started the route; thirty years later, he retired at age forty-seven as one of the youngest mail carriers. In a letter he wrote in 1953, King explained how much he appreciated driving "good horses, which probably compensated partially for lack of salary which was five hundred dollars per year until July 1, 1903, when we got a raise to six hundred dollars." Among the horses he drove were offspring of world-champion trotters. King also told how decent his patrons were to him during the horse-and-buggy days. "There were few days in the winter that I was not invited to have dinner with some of them," he wrote. At one point, when he and his father both had mail routes, his father fell ill for about a month, and Leland delivered both of their mail routes with horses each day.

When Leland King married in 1906, he purchased a home and forty acres at 938 East Sandusky Street in Findlay. It was a one-story house, but Leland added a second story and an attic. Barbara Smith remembers the attic well—it was a play area for her and her many cousins.

As the years went by following his marriage, one word continued to describe his circumstances: deliver. The stork soon delivered three daughters in a matter of a few years, generating the necessity for milk for his family, so Leland bought a cow to fulfill that need. Frequently, the cow produced more milk than the family could drink. Believing in the old adage "waste not, want not," he began offering milk to his postal customers when he delivered the mail. This venture was so successful that he began taking orders from his customers, delivering both milk and mail. The stork delivered four more daughters to King and his wife, and as a result, Leland purchased another cow, leading to more deliveries of milk. Eventually, he had a herd of Jersey cattle—only the Jersey breed would do for Leland King.

Jersey cattle originated on the Isle of Jersey in the Channel Islands off the coast of France. The primary advantages of this breed are its size and production capacity. Because Jerseys are of smaller stature than other breeds (they usually weigh only about nine hundred pounds), they deliver (there's that word again!) their young relatively easily. Statistics also show that Jerseys will mature more quickly and have greater fertility than other kinds of cows. Their milk is apparently superior to any other cow's milk—just ask any Jersey owner. Jersey milk has more of everything: protein, calcium and butterfat.

A 1931 price list on East-View Jersey Farm letterhead shows that Leland King was delivering milk and mail simultaneously. He advertised his wares as "Milk and Cream from Registered Jersey Herd; Tuberculin Free Herd, under Federal Supervision, Findlay, Ohio." The price of a quart of milk was ten cents, and a pint was six cents. He added on the price sheet, however, that "we make a special price on milk to folks who use three quarts or more per day." Additionally, he sold cottage cheese (eighteen cents per pound), cream for coffee (ten cents) or for whipping (twenty cents) and buttermilk.

Leland King began his official dairy business in 1935, two years after he retired from the post office and the same year that his wife, Bertha, the mother of his seven daughters, died after an eighteen-month battle with leukemia, leaving a devastated husband to raise the girls, all of whom were still at home. Eighteen years separated the youngest and oldest King daughters. Barb Smith's mother, the youngest, was only eight years old at the time.

The entire family became involved in the dairy business of the East-View Jersey Farm. The older daughters delivered milk in the early hours of the morning. Barb Smith remembers being amazed that her aunts would get up every morning at 4:00 a.m. to deliver milk before going to school. Just as amazing was the fact that her aunts, as young teenagers, *drove* the milk truck. "They never thought anything of getting up that early," Smith said of her aunts. "Then they'd walk to the high school, which was downtown. And they all had after-school jobs when they were in high school."

Some people chose to stop by the house to pick up their milk from the back porch. "I loved this back porch!" Smith exclaimed, recalling her visits to the house as a child. Although it was enclosed, it was still known as the "back porch" and held sinks, hoses and lots of water, Smith recalled. This was where the girls would bring the milk for their own family use, but friends and neighbors would stop by and purchase milk "on the honor system." A small sign indicated the prices for various items, and the purchaser would simply leave money in a basket.

In 1935, when he began delivering milk from the East-View Jersey Farm operations, Leland purchased a lifetime membership in the American Jersey Cattle Club for fifty dollars and participated in the many activities of the club throughout the years.

When King began his operation in earnest, fifty-seven milk dealers existed in Findlay, a town of about 23,000 people.

King was in the dairy business from 1933 to the late 1940s, when competition began increasing in the area and he was losing his "workforce" to marriage. Although he stayed at the family home until his death in 1962, he purchased an eighty-acre farm near Arcadia as a cash-rent investment. He did not, however, give up his beloved Jerseys. The farmer living on the second farm agreed to take the herd and continue milking them so that Leland could still get his Jersey milk. "Grandpa just had to have his Jersey milk!" exclaimed Smith.

3

IF IT AIN'T THE CHICKEN, IT'S THE FEATHERS

During the 1800s and early 1900s, the poultry "industry" primarily consisted of raising a few chickens in the backyard or perhaps a few hundred on the family farm. Backyard fowl produced eggs for the family and an occasional Sunday chicken dinner, with chicken meat considered a delicacy at the time. In a larger flock of several hundred chickens, farmers could supplement their income by selling eggs, and by the early 1900s, some farmers were also selling "young chickens during the summer for meat as a sideline activity on their family farms. Year-round production was limited because vitamin D had not yet been discovered and the importance of the photoperiod (cycle of sunlight and darkness) and its impact on production was not understood," according to the National Chicken Council. Also, chickens were pretty much on their own when it came to feeding and gaining any kind of nutrition. Unless they were being fattened for that special Sunday dinner, they probably would have searched for whatever scraps they could find. The hen getting the extra buttermilk or grains had no idea that she was being prepped for a dinner.

Weather and housing conditions for poultry led to a 40 percent mortality rate for the birds during the early part of the twentieth century. Poultry lodging amounted to little more than sharing a spot in the barn or another building with other farm animals. Long, cold winters with little or no sunshine may have led to PSAD (Poultry Seasonal Affective Disorder)— just kidding (sort of). Fortunately for the chicks, vitamin D's relationship to disorders such as rickets and osteoporosis was discovered in the 1920s. It was found that vitamin D, or a lack of it, affects chickens in much the same way that it affects humans. The Animal DMV, LLC, website states, "In young chicks, a vitamin D deficiency can cause rickets, resulting in leg and beak deformities. In hens, a vitamin D deficiency adversely affects egg production and can cause calcium deficiency." As farmers began to see the importance of supplementing vitamin D in the diets of their chickens, they also began to see a decrease in the chickens' mortality rate. In fact, today's poultry mortality rates are only around 5 percent.

After the 1920s, hatcheries might have had several different purposes, from selling several dozen eggs to neighbors or area groceries to providing a system of processing and marketing thousands of chickens to consumers throughout the state. Hatcheries in Hancock County during the first half of the twentieth century could be found in Arlington, Findlay, Jenera, Rawson, Van Buren, Vanlue and Mt. Blanchard. Modern Hatcheries in Mt. Blanchard became home to Krout Trucking business but was always known as "the hatchery." According to Ginny Motter, daughter of Gaylord Krout, who started the trucking business, "When we cleaned out the hatchery, we found bills of lading. Crates of chicks from the hatchery went to the depot and were put on a train and sent to Canada!" She also recalled that incubators and boxes for chicks were still in the building when her father bought it. The boxes "were made of mahogany. They were beautiful, airtight. We used them for storage because they were so nice."

DAVIS POULTRY COMPANY—ARLINGTON

When Arlington native Dave Davis begins to relate stories about his family, their businesses, the townspeople and the changes that have taken place throughout the years, his eyes express the love he has for his hometown as much as his soft-spoken voice does. He still lives in the house where he grew up. It was his grandfather's, then his father's and then his, and memorabilia in the form of photographs, yearbooks, sports mementos and countless antiques fill its rooms with the anticipation of tales to be told.

During the early part of the twentieth century, Dave's grandfather, Carl Davis, moved from Mt. Blanchard to Arlington and built a house on Liberty Street. Carl's brother Earl built a house next door. At one point, they decided to go into the egg business and built an addition that became the "egg room." Following that, they built two barns with separate rooflines that were connected by a tunnel. "Trucks sat on the east side of the barn. The kill room, where the chickens were butchered, was on the west side," said Davis. Around 1917, the Davis men partnered with Fred Rothlisberger, who had his own poultry company, eventually becoming D.R. & D. Poultry Company. A 1922 *Arlingtonian* advertisement proclaims: "Wanted. Poultry of All Kinds. Owing to conditions of the market at the present time, we are unable to quote prices on poultry for a week, and will only quote prices for one day at a time. Call us for prices and rest assured you'll get the best the market affords."

The Davises bought Rothlisberger's interest in the business in 1930, as noted in the *Arlingtonian:*

> *Carl L. Davis and son Marvin have purchased the interest of Fred Rothlisberger in the poultry business they have been operating here under the firm name of Davis, Rothlisberger & Davis, and in the future the firm will be known as the Davis Poultry Company. Other interests necessitate Mr. Rothlisberger retiring from the business, which will be carried on by Mr. Davis and Marvin in the same progressive way that has made this firm one of the most popular poultry houses in this section.*

Later, in the mid-1930s, the Davis brothers moved the enterprise to a building on Main Street across from where the fire department stands today.

The new establishment increased the amount of space available for the processing of chickens and eggs. No one remembers which came first. Ba-dump-bump!

As a young boy in the late 1940s and early 1950s, Dave Davis had many fond memories—as well as some "bizarre" ones—of the Davis Poultry Company. He recalled taking trips to Cleveland with his father, Raymond, to deliver truckloads of chickens to a company there. He also remembered the Davis Poultry Company itself: helping at the conveyor belts, watching the women grade the eggs in the egg room, listening to the men in the kill room and slopping hogs at area farms.

Davis told of road trips to Cleveland with his father when Dave was only five or six. The company regularly delivered chickens, both live and processed, to a Cleveland firm, and Dave was sometimes lucky enough to go along. He remembered that ride on State Route 224 as if it were yesterday. Looking out the window of the truck, he watched the farmlands pass by. On each trip, they passed a certain farm "with a milk house cement block on the bottom of a barn, and every time we passed it, my dad was singing

'Cruising Down the River on a Sunday Afternoon.'" That song still evoked strong memories for Dave.

In the slaughter room, Dave watched as workers would "cut the chickens' throats, boil them, put them on a big machine to rip off their feathers and then put them on a table. I remember standing on a steel milk carton helping to sort chickens or doing some other menial jobs," he said. "I must have been eight or nine or ten." He would place the sorted chicken parts on the conveyor belt, where they would then go to the front or east side of the building to be cut into quarters or halves or left whole, then iced and packaged for delivery to grocery stores and other places of business, such as the Findlay Elks Lodge. The chickens were then put in rectangular three- or four-by-two-foot wooden crates. Women on the line would layer ice, paper and chicken in the container. Scales were used to weigh each crate. Women also graded eggs on another conveyor belt with lights under the eggs.

Dave explained an example of the "bizarre" sanitary conditions of the time—the crates were put on the same trucks that had been used to pick up chickens from dusty chicken coops to be taken to grocery stores in Findlay. In 1952, Dave's father, Raymond, became a state employee in the foods and meat inspection department. Dave thought his dad may have had good reason to pursue that position.

On three sides of a big table on the kill floor, men worked cleaning or cutting up chickens. "I can remember them laughing—you can imagine what they were talking about," said Dave. One time, when Reverend Bauman, a German immigrant and the pastor of a local church, was also working there, "probably because he couldn't make enough money as a pastor alone," as Dave put it, in walked a farmer friend, Addi Smith, with a jug of his homemade wine, which he began sharing. Dave continued, "Reverend Bauman took a sip of that wine—they all just passed it around, kind of like communion." And the pastor, in his strong German accent, showed his approval by proclaiming, "Asch gute, Addi!"

Slopping the hogs took on a whole new meaning to Davis. The slaughter room was on the northwest corner of the building. On the floor were, of course, "innards, chicken guts, all over." When he was eight or nine years old, Dave and his uncle Marvin would load barrels filled with chicken guts and other waste onto a truck and head to a hog farm, with Dave in the back of the truck having the time of his life. When they got to a farm, "it was my job to get on the back of the truck and roll the barrels so the stuff would fall out onto the ground," Dave explained. Hogs chased the truck all over the farm, thrilled with their good fortune. "Those hogs knew the sound of the truck and came running."

Davis Poultry was a hot spot on Saturdays, when farmers would come into town to sell eggs or to pick up their checks and then head to the grocery. The front of the building contained an area where they sold gasoline, oil, candy and ice cream. Dave's grandfather Carl would remark, if someone asked him for an ice cream, "The dipper's right there. If you don't get enough, it's your own fault!"

Dave's father, Raymond, who started his new job with the food and meat inspection department in April 1952, spent much of his time in Columbus, leaving the running of the company to Dave's uncle Marvin. Dave admired both his father and his uncle. Marvin had been a two-term mayor of Arlington beginning at age twenty-four—one of the youngest mayors in Ohio. He was also a Hancock County truant officer for several years as well as one of the sixty original state patrolmen.

On Dave's tenth birthday—July 23, 1953—he heard the sad news that his beloved uncle Marvin had died unexpectedly of a heart attack at the age of forty-five. "I'll never forget that. At age ten, I was very impressionable; he and my dad were so much alike; they sounded, acted, walked alike." It was not an easy memory to talk about. Life was never quite the same. But the poultry business, which had been operated by the Davis family for thirty-five years, continued under new management when Walter Morrow bought it and moved the company a short distance west of Arlington to the junction of the cemetery road and the railroad.

PART 2: FROM BOOM TO BUST—FACTORIES

1

GAS FOR GLASS

Free Gas! Free Light! Free Sites! For the Manufacturers Who Will Locate in Findlay!" Thus read the posters and flyers the Findlay Chamber of Commerce began passing out in 1886 to potential businesses that might relocate to Findlay following the discovery of natural gas.

BOOM! In the late nineteenth century, seemingly overnight, Hancock County experienced a gas boom, a manufacturing boom and a land boom. Who could resist an offer of free fuel and land for a new business?

The first commercial gas well in Hancock County was struck in 1884. After a mammoth reservoir of natural gas was finally discovered under Hancock County following speculation that had gone on for decades, industrial companies began flocking to Findlay and the surrounding area, smelling the not-so-sweet odor of cheap success. The population of Findlay grew from a mere 4,633 residents in 1880 to well over 18,000 in 1890, as more and more factories were being built, expanding Findlay's industrial base.

In 1887 alone, more than twenty manufacturing companies built in or relocated to Findlay. Most of the companies that arrived at this time were glass factories, but the Columbia Glass Company had beat the rush by a year.

Located on the east side of the New York Central Railroad on an irregular lot between Ash, Crystal and Walnut Streets in 1886, the Columbia Glass Company had invested $80,000 and then proceeded to do "over $300,000 worth of business during their first season or in about nine months of

This map shows the locations of many of Findlay's glass factories during the 1890s. *Courtesy of the Hancock Historical Museum.*

The Columbia Glass Company factory was located on a lot bordered by Ash, Crystal and Walnut Streets in Findlay. *Courtesy of the Hancock Historical Museum.*

operating time," according to Don E. Smith, a local historian, in *Findlay Pattern Glass*.

Smith also noted: "Was it any wonder that Findlay for a period of twenty-three months, which was from August 1889 to June 1891, had sixteen glass factories in operation simultaneously?" This gave Findlay the distinction of being second only to Pittsburgh in the field of glass production in the United States.

Many types of glass were produced in the Findlay glass factories, including window glass, tableware or flint glass, bottles, lamp chimneys and novelties. Smith describes the tableware factories as being "substantially built of brick and stone with metal roofs. They were built to last many years." However, the window glass factories were more often constructed of wood, much like a large barn.

Although many glass factories were located throughout Findlay, most of them naturally arose near railroad lines. In 1876, Bellaire Goblet Works, originally from Bellaire, Ohio, moved to Findlay and located on Bolton Avenue between Davis and College Streets and along the Cincinnati, Hamilton & Dayton Railway switch. A few blocks north, but also along the tracks and Bolton Avenue, were the Dalzell, Gilmore & Leighton Glass Company; the Clay Pot Works; and the Model Glass Works. In the northern part of Findlay, east of North Main Street near Tioga and Stanley Streets and along the Toledo, Columbus & Cincinnati Railroad, stood the Findlay Flint Glass Works and the United Glass Company. The Globe and Chimney Works at East Main Cross and North Blanchard Avenue was not far from the Indiana, Bloomington & Western Railway. Columbia Glass, Buckeye Window Glass and Findlay Window Glass were on either side of the two intersecting railway lines near Crystal Avenue and Walnut Street.

The Dalzell, Gilmore & Leighton Glass Company—Findlay

It was not long after the discovery of natural gas in Hancock County and the offers of free (or at least substantially less expensive) fuel that the Dalzell Brothers & Gilmore Glass Company moved from Wellsburg, West Virginia, where it had begun in 1884, to a large site in northwest Findlay. The conditions of the deal, set by the Howard and Swing land syndicates, included a free four-acre lot for the purpose of building the factory and free gas for five years. On top of that, the Dalzell Brothers & Gilmore Glass Company would receive a cash bonus. All the glass company had to do was build a $60,000 factory and hire no fewer than three hundred people to work in it.

In September 1888, the *Findlay Weekly Republican* reported about this "New Industry" coming to Findlay: the Dalzell, Gilmore & Leighton Glass Company. "Yesterday the first of the three eleven-pot furnaces at the flint glass works of the Dalzell, Gilmore & Leighton Co., on the Wyoming Place Addition, began work with about one hundred employees, seventy-five of whom just got here from Wellsburg, West Virginia. A hundred more men are expected tomorrow and within a few weeks it is hoped to have the full force of three hundred and fifty men at work, with three furnaces in operation."

On the same day, the *Hancock Courier* also reported on the "largest glass house in Northwestern Ohio." This article detailed some other aspects of the company:

> *The institution is an old and well-established one, with its business connections found throughout the country. Its specialties are tableware and lamp goods, of a high class. A number of expert engravers and cutters are employed, and a different class of work produced than is attempted at any of the others. The buildings are all of brick, covering an immense area, and the firm claim they have the best arranged and most complete glass house in this country.*

Work had begun. And just as quickly, work was stopped. In October 1888, some twenty boys went on strike, demanding that their wages be raised from fifty cents to sixty cents per day. The company refused and countered that the sixty-cent amount was greater than what was being paid "anywhere in the country." It seems, though, that the boys had not entered into this arrangement on their own. There was talk about some "bums from Wheeling" who may have "persuaded and intimidated" the boys into striking with them. The workers who remained were not happy with the boys who caused them to lose a day's pay, but everyone who wanted to work at the old price—even those who were striking—would be permitted to do so, manager W.A.B. Dalzell assured them.

It was not unusual to have young boys employed at the area factories at this time. Depending on the work, much of which was light, young teens could easily handle the job. The Dalzell factory frequently advertised for boys to work in the factory, sometimes for as many as fifty boys at a time,

The Dalzell, Gilmore & Leighton Glass Company built a factory in northwest Findlay in 1888. *Courtesy of the Hancock Historical Museum.*

and when the company couldn't get enough youngsters from the nearby area, it often arranged to have orphans transported to the area to work. The company had done this in Wellsburg, and it proved necessary to elicit help from eastern orphanages to staff the factory in Findlay.

In November 1888, an Associated Press article out of Boston landed in the *Hancock Courier* regarding possible employment of boys under the age of twelve at some Ohio glass factories. The boys were from St. John's Home in Boston. Mother de Chantel, from St. John's, assured the Boston reporter that she had known glass-factory owners from both the Nickel Plate Glass Company in Fostoria and the Dalzell, Gilmore & Leighton Glass Company in Findlay for many years: "I have been in the works at both places and saw that if the boys could be induced to work there, it would be better to have them do so and learn a useful trade, and not grow up in idleness." She continued to explain that she had even stayed with the boys where they were being housed in Fostoria for several days. "They were well treated, well fed and lodged and their work was clean and light."

As for the claim of hiring underage boys, Mother de Chantel said that she had known of only one case where a boy under twelve was sent to Ohio, and it was by mistake. Large for his age, the boy had actually been only eleven and a half years old. When Mother de Chantel discovered this error, she immediately ordered him back to Boston and sent a thirteen-year-old replacement. She reiterated that it was important for these boys to have a fair chance at creating a future for themselves: "They cannot learn a trade or business in St. John's Home and they can learn a useful trade there," she added. "When they left, we gave them each two suits of clothing, four shirts, four suits of underclothing, four pairs of socks, a good pair of shoes and a hat, so they will scarcely want anything for several months at least."

When a *Courier* reporter contacted the Dalzell factory regarding the story, he was told that the information was essentially correct. The thirty boys who had recently arrived were already at work. In addition to learning a practical skill, the boys were able to live together in rented housing with a matron to oversee their well-being.

The following February, the *Weekly Jeffersonian* reported, "Messrs. Dalzell, Gilmore, and Leighton furnished the thirty orphan boys in their employ with fine new dress suits so that they could properly observe the Sabbath. Lippman's Clothing House was awarded the contract. Much credit to Messrs. Dalzell, Gilmore & Leighton for the liberal manner in which they house and clothe the little fellows."

Just as the Dalzell brothers had had their own gas well on their property near Wellsburg, so did the Dalzell, Gilmore, & Leighton Glass Company in Findlay acquire its own well. In January 1889, the land syndicate drilled a well that "will furnish this large concern with an abundance of the grandest fuel on earth for glass making." Little did management know that time was running out on the "inexhaustible" supply of natural gas; however, W.A.B. Dalzell, company manager, was smart enough to prepare plan B and plan C in case the gas no longer supplied enough fuel.

In January 1893, the plant added $4,000 of crude oil burners to parts of the plant that had depended on natural gas. As Don E. Smith wrote, "When the city shut off the gas to the glass factories, Dalzells turned on their oil burners and never missed a melt."

But crude oil was expensive, so later that year, the Dalzell, Gilmore, & Leighton factory began using coal as well as natural gas to fuel its furnaces, and the opening of new railroad lines aided in lowering the rate on coal being shipped to the area. The Toledo & Ohio Central completed an extension from Columbus to Findlay in 1887. According to an article in the *Daily Courier* in November 1893, coal was "cheap as gas." A representative from the railroad met with manufacturers in Findlay, quoting a rate for coal per ton that was well received. Although the rates were "not for publication," the reporter apparently knew someone who knew someone and subsequently printed the prices that disclosed the comparison of gas to coal, with coal being decidedly less expensive:

It is estimated that it takes 26,000 cubic feet of gas to equal one ton of coal. At the present price of 5 cents per thousand cubic feet, charged to the factories, this would make the gas which equals a ton of coal, cost $1.30, or 25 cents more than a ton of coal. It will thus be seen that the coal rate is placed at a low point that is especially encouraging to manufacturers and will enable them to thrive and prosper.

Dalzell, Gilmore & Leighton jumped on the bandwagon and began converting one of its furnaces to burn coal. In August 1894, the company had run the new furnace for about a week. "The apparatus works finely with natural gas," the *Hancock Courier* reported, "and it is thought will do still better with coal. One of the old furnaces is also being operated. The other one will be torn down at once, to be rebuilt with the coal-gas system." As a result, many more men were employed at the factory.

A *Findlay Republican* reporter was granted a tour of the Dalzell plant by W.A.B. Dalzell in July 1899 and enlightened the reader, in great detail, about exactly how the factory operated.

First and foremost, the reporter explained, "the essentials for a glass factory are good and cheap fuel, and a pure white sand." Besides this sand, or silicon dioxide, pure sodium carbonate (soda), calcium oxide (lime) and other substances such as arsenic, manganese and cobalt are necessary. The white sand came from Illinois. The soda had formerly come from abroad, but due to the McKinley Tariff of 1892, a five-dollar duty was put on the soda. Since the factory used more than three hundred tons of soda per year, management was able to obtain the material from a couple of new plants in New York and Michigan. Chile saltpeter, also known as sodium nitrate, was shipped from large nitrate beds in Chile and Bolivia. Arsenic came from Germany, with other nations contributing many of the more minor ingredients.

The Dalzell plant fashioned many different and unique glass items, including lamps, tableware, vases and globes. Something that many people probably did not realize is that these items went in and out of style just as clothing or furniture might. Therefore, what was wildly popular one year might have absolutely no appeal the next, or what was a successful seller in one region might not move in another.

Regular flint glass was made from a variety of ingredients mixed and layered in long box-shaped tanks in a mixing room. "A layer of sand is spread over the bottom and on it a layer of soda and then one of lime, together with the other necessary ingredients, all of which have been mixed." Then this went into the furnace to melt.

Molding and blowing are two techniques used in the creation of lamps. The lamp bowl began as molten glass and was put into a mold and then blown, with pressure allowing it to take the shape of the mold. From there, the rough lamp, which was still very hot, went to an oven, slowly passing from a high heat to a much cooler temperature. Rough edges were filed and a collar put on the neck of the lamp to create a leakproof joint.

So many of the lamps and vases and other products from Dalzell, Gilmore & Leighton exhibited beautiful ornamentation. The ornaments could be created by etching or by cutting, with cutting being more "artistic and widely used."

Men, women, boys and girls worked at this factory. In 1899, 40 of the 225 employees were women and girls. Their roles included "sorting, cleaning, finishing, decorating and packing the various articles that are turned out."

Dalzell, Gilmore & Leighton glassware was shipped throughout the United States and to other countries, including Mexico and Australia. The *Findlay Republican* article summarized: "This firm has been one of the most valuable and reliable of the industries of Findlay and has contributed in no small way to the prosperity of the city."

Some of the names of the Dalzell glass pieces are as beautiful or unusual as the glass itself. "Bringing Home the Cows," on a large pitcher, showed a detailed pastoral scene featuring cows, a fence, trees and other wildlife. Another pitcher, "Bicycle Girl," displayed a carefree young girl wearing a Victorian-style dress while riding a bike. "Teardrop with Eyewinkers," a kerosene lamp, delicately incorporated several different shapes into its design. The "Eyewinker" motif was made in several different colors "from time to time." All of these pieces exhibited the artistic talent that was a part of the Dalzell, Gilmore & Leighton Glass Company.

Other types of glassware made at the plant included pressed, cut and etched pieces. The crystal-pressed Priscilla pattern made by the Dalzell plant continued to be produced after the National Glass Company bought out the company. Dalzell's Columbia pattern was known as a pie-crust glass because the edges were crimped in the same way a baker might crimp the edges of a pie crust.

Throughout its tenure in Findlay, Ohio, this glass factory had its share of setbacks, including theft, weather damage and accidents. In January 1890, the *Hancock Courier* noted, "The Dalzell, Gilmore & Leighton Co. have made important discoveries, showing where a considerable amount of missing glassware has gone to. A detective has discovered that some of

This "Bringing Home the Cows" water pitcher, made by the Dalzell, Gilmore & Leighton Glass Company, exhibits wonderful detail. *Courtesy of the Hancock Historical Museum.*

The "Bicycle Girl" water pitcher is an example of the Dalzell, Gilmore & Leighton Glass Company's glassware. *Courtesy of the Hancock Historical Museum.*

the workingmen have been taking the ware home with them, in some cases accumulating quite a quantity of it. It is not positive whether there will be any prosecution."

An almost-catastrophic accident occurred on the evening of June 24, 1891, when "the immense ten-foot fly-wheel on the engine in the glass factory of the Dalzell, Gilmore & Leighton company burst into a thousand pieces and flew with terrible force through the roof of the building, many of the pieces then falling back into the factory." Although many workers were in the area of the engine, none of them were seriously injured, probably as a result of the wheel going through the roof first. When pieces of the wheel fell back into the factory, though, much of the glassware being stored there was broken. The sixty-horsepower engine did not fare so well, either, and was considered a total loss.

Several years later, in 1900, another part of the Dalzell plant experienced a freakish accident. A vicious wind storm raged through Findlay, causing major damage and injury at the glass factory. The *Weekly Jeffersonian* described the storm as the "perfect hurricane. The wind was quite warm, however, and did not greatly inconvenience the people"— except at the Dalzell, Gilmore & Leighton Glass Company. The storm blew a 25,000-gallon water tank from its derrick, and it hit the iron roof and squashed the wooden structure of the decorating building. "Quite a number of girls and men were at work in the building at the time, nearly all of whom were more or less injured."

Area doctors examined the injured, and five people were sent home via ambulance. Many of the four hundred employees worked quickly to rescue those who had been trapped in the building. The *Jeffersonian* continued: "W.A.B. Dalzell, the manager, gave the physicians orders to have all the injured properly taken care of. Of course, the order was obeyed." Injuries included compound fractures, cuts and bruises, but no injuries so serious as to require a hospital stay. The monetary loss on the building and tank amounted to between $500 and $600. The wooden water tank, like Humpty Dumpty, couldn't be put back together again, but plans were soon drawn up to reconstruct a tank as soon as possible. The decorating building also had to be rebuilt. However, the factory was not going to be operational for much longer.

In late 1900, Dalzell, Gilmore & Leighton stockholders held a meeting, resolving to discontinue as a corporation. As all of the business debts had been paid, it was agreed that the remaining assets would be split among the stockholders. The *Findlay Union* predicted that "the first of the new year the

Today, a building supply company occupies the land on Bolton Avenue between Madison and Rockwell Avenues where the Dalzell, Gilmore & Leighton Glass Company once stood. *Courtesy of the Hancock Historical Museum.*

Dalzell glass house will quench its fires and the plant dismantled and the men transferred to the plant at Cambridge."

The *Union* was correct and informed its readers in February 1902: "The Dalzell glass plant is a thing of the past, the last employees left Monday for Cambridge. It is too bad for Findlay to lose an establishment of this kind and we hope it will not be long before there is a factory of equal magnitude to take its place."

The National Glass Company had purchased the Dalzell, Gilmore & Leighton Glass Company in November 1901 for $200,000 cash. W.A.B. Dalzell became the superintendent of this factory and was "to run the plant as if it were his own." A short time later, Dalzell took charge of all of the National Glass Company's plants in Ohio.

2

DRAINING THE SWAMP

The earliest endeavors of clearing and draining fields consisted of digging a ditch by hand and directing the surface water away to a stream or nearby river. Not only would farmers have to drain the surface water, they would also have to drain the subsurface water. Neither of these tasks were simple. According to Jim Mollenkopf's book *The Great Black Swamp*, "The first underdrains were crude, usually stones or saplings laid in a trench and covered over. These drains were gradually replaced by a longer-lasting technique of nailing two planks into a V and laying them inverted in a trench and covering them over."

This type of draining took place in the 1840s and '50s, when shipping drainage tiles from other areas to northwest Ohio was prohibitively expensive. Mollenkopf states, "It was discovered around 1860 that a tremendous bed of clay lay under the rich topsoil of the Swamp, and by 1880, dozens of tile factories had sprung up in the Black Swamp counties."

One of the earliest area attempts to successfully drain farmland took place around 1860 in Jackson Township in the southern part of the county. Evan Dorsey Stevenson had moved to Hancock County a few years earlier to settle the estate of his late father, who had owned 120 acres of land. About 45 acres in the highest part of the parcel had been cleared, and a cabin had been built. Stevenson proceeded to drain off as much surface water as he could by digging a ditch. *A Centennial Biographical History of Hancock County, Ohio*, describes this as "the first ditch in the township and was the beginning of systematic drainage here." Although many people thought he was simply "burying his money" with this "nonsense," Stevenson proved them wrong. The fall after his initial tiling, he was able to sell his cornfield for twenty-five dollars per acre. "At once others began laying tile, until today (1903) the county is well tiled and drained."

By the mid-1880s, most of Hancock County's communities and/or townships had established tile-producing factories. In Blanchard Township in western Hancock County, Lewis Dukes Sr. began a tile factory on his farm. As Robert. C. Brown wrote, "The greater portion of the flat lands has been brought under a high state of cultivation by a plentiful use of the tile made in this factory, and thus the wealth of the township has been annually increased and multiplied." He added that "the productiveness of the lands here is largely due to the judicious use of tiles, and this factory has therefore been of inestimable value to the farmers of Blanchard Township."

In Allen Township, north of Findlay, Wallace Dorsey made a career change after twenty years as a carpenter. In 1835, he had purchased a government tract (land in a wild state) of 160 acres, located in Allen and Cass Townships, and was able to develop it into a successful farm. Adding 20 acres to his farm in 1863, he saw that he would need to pay more attention to farming and less to carpentry. This led him into manufacturing drainage tile, beginning in 1877, not only for himself but for others in need of the product. *A Centennial Biographical History* points out: "He supplies an extensive trade with tile of various sizes and quality, and the business has proved quite lucrative to the proprietor, as well as an accommodation to the large class in need of this indispensable aid to drainage."

William Pendleton began manufacturing tile in Blanchard Township before moving to Putnam County and doing the same. He returned to Pleasant Township in Hancock County in 1881 and continued to make brick and tile. In 1884, he established the McComb Tile and Brick Works. Robert C. Brown, in his history of Hancock County, describes the plant as "fitted up with all the modern improvements in this line, worked by steam, the industry gives work to several men and the works have a capacity for turning out 400,000 tiles annually."

Other communities with tile factories or brickyards during the 1880s included Washington Township (Arcadia), Cory (today's Mt. Cory), Deweyville, Rawson and Vanlue.

Before the advent of mechanical ditchers, men carried out the unenviable task of digging drainage ditches using only picks, shovels and muscle power. But James B. Hill changed all of that with the introduction of his steam-powered traction ditcher. This invention, patented in 1894, revolutionized the industry of laying drainage tile. An article from the American Society of Mechanical Engineers describes this mammoth machine: "The steam-driven ditcher cut in a single motion along a consistent gradient and was operated by two laborers. These machines replaced slow and costly hand labor."

Hill had lived in Bowling Green, Deshler and Carey before moving in 1902 to Findlay, where the Van Buren, Heck and Marvin Foundry began manufacturing these steam-powered machines. By 1910, around seven hundred of the machines had been built and shipped. A refurbished Buckeye Traction Ditcher from 1902 is on display at the Hancock Historical Museum.

Tile Companies—Arlington, Rawson, McComb

The twentieth century ushered in many innovations, including improved tile factories. Many of the newspapers of the time expressed hopes that a tile factory would be located in their respective communities. In March 1910, the *Arlingtonian* reported, "There is a movement afoot to get a cement tile factory here. The sample of tiles made by the machine, lately invented for that purpose, can be seen at the Ohio Hardware. There is loose capital plenty of it about Arlington to establish some kind of a tile factory and no enterprise would be of more benefit to town and community."

A plant opened in Arlington that year. By September, the newspaper's editor had paid a visit to the new plant. He was impressed, finding "the boys busy making tile to 'beat the band.'" He seemed almost overwhelmed by the newness of the building (made from their own cement blocks) and the machinery used to create the tile. Employing eight or nine men when the factory opened, the company assured the public that more workers would soon be added, as the orders for tile were quickly coming in.

The prevailing attitude from cement tile makers at this time was that cement tiles were superior to clay tiles. A notice in a February 1911 *Arlingtonian* gave the reader several reasons to buy Arlington Cement Tile: "Cement tile being of uniform shape are easy to lay, make the nicest looking drain, and have the greatest water-carrying capacity." They resist frost action, they don't crumble, and when hit with metal, they won't deteriorate.

This factory had several owners and eventually became a building and supply enterprise. By 1922, the company not only made cement tile but had also added the production of concrete blocks for use in house construction.

Don Steinman wrote of the Arlington Cement Tile Factory in an issue of the ECHO (Eagle Creek Historical Organization) newsletter. In the 1940s, the business now known as the Arlington Builders and Supply Company was being run by Charles Gehrisch and his son-in-law Carl Traucht. Concrete blocks had become popular for creating house foundations, but in 1945, the company built two concrete block houses "on spec." One sat on the northeast corner of Main and Wilch Streets, and the other was at the southern corner of Cumberland and West Liberty Streets. Steinman noted, "the building across the street, which for many years housed the J.G. Bame Implement Company and currently the Smith-Heldman Insurance and the Arlington VFW, is thought to be the only other building in town built with block from the local plant."

Steinman found the process of making cement tile and concrete blocks quite interesting. "It took two men to run the tile-making machine," he wrote. Materials needed for making the tile were cement, crushed stone and sand. Cement was hand fed into a steel metal jacket, and an auger "came up from the bottom of the machine and took much of the cement out of the center, creating the hole in the tile." The jacket was then removed, and the tiles were placed on racks and moved to the kiln room, where the blocks were steam cured for two days. Finally, the finished tiles were moved outside, taken off the racks and stacked. "This was not a hazardous job," said Steinman, "but yellow palm gloves did not last long at all and the workers had to buy their own gloves. Soles of shoes also wore out fast."

In contrast, the concrete block machine dumped a mix from one hopper to another and tamped it down, then the block was cleaned off before being placed on a conveyor belt. Workers had to remove the blocks from the conveyor by hand. And these blocks were heavy, ranging from forty-five to fifty-five pounds, depending on type.

Due to competition from area tile makers, the cement tile factory in Arlington only lasted until the late 1940s.

Newspapers also encouraged the small town of Rawson to construct a tile factory, chiding landowners to stop being "so reluctant about letting loose of their property at a fair value," according to the *Republican Jeffersonian* in January 1908. Again, the newspaper seems to have convinced the good people of the area that the time was ripe for investing in the tile business.

A June 1909 *Hancock Courier* praised the Rawson Tile Company for having "the best modern tile making plant in the county and one of the best in the state, and that fact coupled with the fact that the plant has a superior quality of clay insures the company success and guarantees to the

Employees stand by the tile factory in Rawson, which operated in the early part of the twentieth century. *Courtesy of the Hancock Historical Museum.*

farmers in this part of the county a make of tile second to none anywhere in the country."

The reporter attended the dedication of the tile factory and described the event in glowing terms: "The interior of the building was neatly arranged and well-illuminated and while the moon with a smiling visage shed her radiance over the face of nature, three hundred and twenty-five of the good natured and kindly disposed citizens of Rawson and vicinity assembled on the grounds of the interior of the plant." Attendees enjoyed speeches, poems, ice cream and cake—what better way to celebrate the inception of Rawson's newest factory?

In October 1914, the *Hancock Courier* reported that the Rawson tile mill had had "one of the most profitable seasons in its history. Under the capable and energetic management of W.A. Barger, the mill year has been filled with first class tile of various sizes."

Barger was also instrumental as a machine operator in a McComb tile mill, as reported in the November 1914 *Hancock Courier*. "Mr. Barger is the energetic young man who so successfully managed the Rawson tile mill during the summer and filled up the yard there with a first-class product."

Not unlike Arlington, McComb had a tile mill in the late nineteenth and early twentieth century and beyond. George Glaser, a businessman who lived in McComb, operated the McComb Tile Works beginning in the late 1940s. As an ad read, "For Land's Sake! Use concrete drain tile made at McComb Tile Works." The business ran well until one night in February 1953, when a fire raged through the plant. A neighbor discovered the fire and alerted her husband, who called the village fire department. Not only was the tile plant destroyed, but a large barn, a concrete outbuilding, all of the machinery, nearly three hundred barrels of cement and six thousand tiles were lost.

George Glaser and his wife, who were vacationing in Florida at the time, returned early the following week. Their son, Richard, had been running the business in their absence and was injured while trying to retrieve a lift truck full of tile from the flames. He suffered severe burns on his hands but was successful in saving at least some of the products. Estimated losses were between $25,000 and $30,000, with about $10,000 of that from the machinery. About a third of the loss was covered by insurance.

But that was not the end of McComb Tile Works, for the business was rebuilt and continued to supply concrete tile to area farmers for many more years.

HANCOCK BRICK & TILE—FINDLAY

Daniel E. Child was a true entrepreneur—a man who had a gift for finding needs and filling them. In the 1880s, at the beginning of the gas and oil boom, Daniel Child and his family moved to Findlay from Dayton, where Daniel had worked in a variety of businesses, selling sewing machines and musical instruments, after having spent several years teaching grade school and college, always meeting the needs of others.

Once he was established in Findlay, he became involved in many different ventures. This is not to say that he flitted from one thing to another out of boredom or failing; he simply saw other needs that had to be filled.

Findlay had at least eight brickyards when Daniel came to town. He must have noticed that even with that many brickyards or factories, Findlay and Hancock County needed more to fulfill the demand for brick. In January 1888, the *Daily Courier* reported: "Another new brick yard will be started here soon. Although many millions of brick were used in building last year, nearly as many have already been contracted for the coming season's work, while many others who contemplate building are just getting their plans drawn and have not yet put in their orders."

The following year, George Dorney, Daniel Child and John Murray formed Dorney, Child & Murray, a firm with the stated purpose of manufacturing pressed brick and common brick. An 1890 Sanborn Fire Insurance map of Findlay shows the "Dorney, Childs [*sic*] & Murray Brick Yard" on the south side of East Yates Avenue in southeast Findlay; it also included a brick shed and five-foot-high brick racks. A boardinghouse was erected nearby for company employees.

The Child & Murray Tile Factory (Dorney had since left the firm) then became what one Findlay newspaper called the "LARGEST [factory] IN OHIO." It was March 1892, and a *Findlay Union* reporter "visited these gentlemen at their factory and was really astonished to see what an immense plant they have established and are maintaining." The company had been manufacturing "a superior quality of building brick" for several years during the summer, shipping over one hundred carloads throughout the area. But that was seasonal, and they wanted to create a facility that would run year-round, so they bought more land "with the finest clay ground in this county" and added a new tile factory.

A four-story brick "dry house" with a 20,000-square-foot floor area, able to dry 180,000 three-inch tiles simultaneously, was located on the east side of the Toledo, Columbus & Cincinnati Railroad tracks. The fifty-six-square-foot machine/workroom housed the "latest and most improved" equipment, making it the only factory capable of producing large twenty- and twenty-four-inch tiles for public ditches. Other tiles made there were between eight and twenty-four inches in diameter. The factory had three "up and down draft" kilns, with a fourth under construction. In addition, a large shed was attached to the machine room, and another tarpaper-roofed shed was connected to the main building. One shed held the boiler, the engine, the brick machine and the tile machine. A kiln for burning tile was situated beside the main building, as well, and the brick kiln was several hundred feet away from the building. As far as brick production went, the factory already had over a million bricks ready for the spring market.

During the previous year, 1891, Child and Murray had successfully drilled for natural gas on their property, thus adding a cost-saving element to the business. The kilns could be fired and the tiles dried through the fuel supplied by this well all year long, no matter what the weather brought. The kilns continuously fired at temperatures between 1200°F and 1500°F, making for a blisteringly hot workplace. The threat of fire pervaded, but employees knew the risk and continued to work on the task at hand.

In the wee hours of September 9, 1892, the risk became a reality. The *Daily Courier* reported: "At 3:30 o'clock this morning the sounding of the fire alarm from box 81 and the persistent shrieks of the steam whistles from several factories, announced that a fire was in progress at the South End, and this was soon confirmed by the lurid light which flamed up to the sky as though the demons of destruction were holding high carnival in mad glee at destroying the hard work of man's hands." Yes, it was the almost-new Child & Murray Tile Factory that burned throughout the night. The fire had started in the shed roof from the boiler's smokestack and quickly spread. The dozen or so men on the night shift, most of them on the fourth floor of the building, saw the flames through a window "and rushed down to try to extinguish the flames with buckets of water, but their efforts were without avail." An alarm was sounded, but it was already too late.

Because the fire department was so far away from this south-end factory, the time it took firefighters to get there meant little could be done to save the buildings and much of the stock. Co-owner John Murray had been telephoned at his First Street home about the fire and arrived around the same time as the fire engine and began directing the firefighters where to aim the water hose. "A line of hose two thousand feet in length was stretched to Eagle creek, the only available source of water supply, and a stream of water directed on the building, but without avail," the article continued. "The roof soon fell in, and the timbers of the floors were burned and fell in, letting their great loads of valuable material fall with them into the seething caldron of fire below."

Murray stood near the north side of the shed and continued to direct the firemen, when "suddenly the timbers supporting the brick work gave way, and he was buried beneath the falling wall." He was placed on a stretcher and transported to his home by a patrol wagon. Head, neck, ankle and internal injuries, as well as severe burns, left him with little hope for recovery. He died on the afternoon of September 12, leaving behind a wife and three young sons.

In addition to the material loss of machinery, buildings and tile, the Child & Murray Tile Factory and the whole of Hancock County lost a man who was "kind to his neighbors, honest in his business relations, a model husband and loving father," according to Murray's obituary in the *Findlay Union* on September 15, 1892.

Daniel Child, who had been out of town the night of the fire, wasted no time in gearing up another factory. The November 26, 1892 Findlay *Morning Republican* noted:

D.E. Child is rebuilding his tile factory and in addition a new boiler house and workshop. He has been working twenty-five men every day and will have ten masons at work from now till the work is finished. The new plant will be better built and more expansive than the old one was and will be ready for operation soon after the new year, if the weather continues favorable. Mr. Child has plenty of gas from his own well and is burning a kiln of 350,000 brick. In his new plant he can make brick as well as tile in winter.

Child spent the next decade working in the brick and tile industry. By the early 1900s, he was ready to start an even bigger and better business and created the Hancock Brick & Tile Company. Also at this time, his sons D Earl and J. Leo entered into the business with their father. A third son, Roy Burton, operated his own contracting business in Findlay. [An aside: When asked about the curious names containing initials and middle names, E. Tom Child, grandson of Daniel Child, replied, "My father was D—no dot!" D Earl seems to be the only "dotless" Child, though most of the male members of the family retain the first initial–middle name appellation.]

The new factory was located about two blocks south of the old Child & Murray brickyard. The plant on Olive Avenue covered about twenty acres and was situated about a half mile from the clay pit. Remnants of the clay pits survive today as a pond where many Findlay residents have enjoyed ice skating or fishing.

By 1906, this plant was definitely prospering, although it had been successful for several years—sometimes too successful. On occasion, the factory had more orders than it could supply to the Hancock County area, let alone orders from more distant places. In February 1906, the *Findlay Republican Courier* reported: "From thirty to thirty-five wagons from the rural districts in this county visit the plant daily and haul away tile. This trade alone was equal to the capacity of the plant almost and was the direct means of causing the plant to get sixty cars behind on their shipping orders." This led to establishing a night crew, with twenty of the company's sixty employees working through the night. The company also laid its own track from the factory to the clay pits to improve the efficiency of the clay-hauling process.

An example of the Child family's community spirit could be seen during a damaging flood in 1913. Findlay has withstood many, many floods before that time and since. The Blanchard River, which runs through the heart of the city, and Eagle Creek inundate buildings, businesses and abodes when at flood stage. Even though the Hancock Brick & Tile factory suffered damage from rising waters over the years, the business made sure that other area residents were provided for during these times. In 1913, Hancock Brick & Tile donated groceries, coal and other provisions to those affected by the flood and its aftermath.

The following year, Daniel Child turned over complete operations to his sons D Earl and J. Leo, although he maintained his position on the board of directors until his death in 1917.

The Roaring Twenties found the Hancock Brick & Tile Company thriving, as vividly portrayed in an article in a 1925 *Hancock County Herald*: "In the solving of the problems of the day there is no profession that has come into prominence more in the past few years than that of the drain tile manufacturer and distributor and in this respect, we desire to refer you to this well-known firm, which has greatly aided in the progress of the country."

During the 1920s and early 1930s, Hancock Brick & Tile began expanding and acquiring other tile factories in Ohio, Indiana and Michigan. In 1928, Hancock Brick & Tile bought the E. Biglow tile plant in New London, Ohio, about seventy miles east of Findlay. That plant eventually switched from using clay, which was scarce in that part of Ohio, to creating tiles using more readily available shale, which had been discovered only a couple of miles from the New London facility. During World War II and shortly thereafter,

A truck loaded with tile from the Hancock Brick & Tile Company in Findlay is ready to make deliveries. *Courtesy of the Hancock Historical Museum.*

this facility employed German and Italian prisoners of war housed at Camp Perry near Sandusky, Ohio.

Continuing to operate even during the difficult times of the Great Depression, Hancock Brick & Tile endured and grew, acquiring more factories, and was the sole owner of all of its subsidiaries by 1940.

One afternoon in 2018, E. Tom Child, age ninety-nine, sat in his book-filled home and talked about Hancock Brick & Tile, living for nearly ten decades and surviving the attack on Pearl Harbor. His daughter, Sue Child, added her memories, too.

As a junior high student in the 1930s, E. Tom spent his summers working at the Hancock Brick & Tile plant. "I enjoyed working with people," he said, explaining that the men working in the factory were "always free speaking, always had time for a visit." One thing he recalled was the men's use of mittens with two thumbs—not one—in working with dry product. The tile was not only terribly hot coming out of the kiln but also extremely abrasive. To protect their hands, workers wore two-thumbed mittens. "Most men went through two pair a day," he related. "They [the mittens, not the men] had thumbs on both sides so that you could turn them over," thus doubling the effectiveness of each mitten.

After high school, E. Tom attended Ohio Wesleyan for one year, then transferred to Ohio State. At the conclusion of his second year, he received an offer to attend a "fast track" program to become an officer in the Naval Reserve. As Sue put it, "Only the 'good guys' got those telegrams."

He signed up on August 13, 1940, "and as soon as I got in the school and a commission, it was way better than back at work!" The U.S. Navy paid him $125 a month, while he had only earned about a third of that amount at the family business: 42.5¢ per day. And he was surprised that "raises" came every few months in the navy rather than every couple of years, as in civilian companies.

In 1946, after his return to Findlay following his tour of duty in the Pacific, E. Tom Child, son of D Earl, and his cousin James L. Child Jr. (son of J. Leo) took over the management of Hancock Brick & Tile, but all four shared in the decision-making for the company.

The factory itself was rebuilt and updated in the 1950s following another fire and continued to be a leader in brick and tile manufacturing. Although the plant was newer, the process was still essentially the same as it had been fifty years earlier. A July 1962 *Findlay Republican Courier* article describes the method:

This Hancock Brick & Tile Company display was part of the 1962 Fort Findlay Sesquicentennial celebration.

The raw material, a special type of clay found in only a few sections of the country, is particularly adaptable to the production of clay tile. It is transported either by private railway or truck to the plant where it is processed, by being run through a large gas-fired rotary grinder. It is dried, pulverized and all foreign matter removed. It then goes into large clay tanks, or silos, from which it feeds to the manufacturing rooms. It is mixed in water under vacuum to remove all the air. The tile is extruded or pushed out and placed into tunnels or a drying room. After reaching the proper degree of dryness, it is taken to the gas-fired kilns where it is burned. The final product is then transported to locations throughout the country for consumer use.

The production of clay tile at Hancock Brick & Tile lasted until 1970, although sales and delivery continued for some time. According to a 1974 *Findlay Republican Courier* article, "the 15 cylindrical kilns were shut down in

July 1970 as the plant went exclusively to the manufacture of plastic tubing for underground drainage."

The implementation of plastics led to the demise of the clay drainage tile industry and the creation of a new Findlay industry called Hancor (Hancock Corrugated). Instead of clay tile, this new company produced polyethylene plastic tubing. The rationale? Plastic tubing is lighter than clay tile, so it's cleaner, less energy is used to create it and it's easier to transport than tile.

In 1978, the D Earl side of the family sold its share of the company to the J. Leo side, thus ending E. Tom's tenure with the company. When asked when—or if—he had retired, he replied, "Oh, my. Well, I was always with the clay and brick business. I got away from plastic piping. Hancock Brick & Tile was always clay pipe. A real place."

3

HEADS AND MEDS

For almost every type of factory in Findlay and Hancock County that produced common, everyday necessities like glassware, drainage tile and furniture, there were just as many factories being established to meet more unusual needs. Findlay had its share of places that manufactured more extraordinary—or at the very least, unexpected—products. Who knew Findlay had a beef hoist factory (and what is a beef hoist, anyway)? Or a bicycle factory? How about a casket factory? Or horseradish, perfume and piano factories? Typewriters and umbrellas? Yes, Findlay was home to all of these manufacturers—and then some.

Just to ease your mind a bit, a beef hoist is what it sounds like: a piece of machinery designed to allow one person, usually a butcher, to lift a beef carcass for easier carving of the beef into various portions. Findlay's beef hoist factory was started in 1891 by W.C. Treece. At that time, the factory could produce up to ten full hoists in one day, and the completed outfits were shipped throughout the United States and to other countries. The hoists were fourteen feet high and required over twenty-three feet of three-quarter-inch rope.

In 1932, the Findlay *Morning Republican* featured an article about the Treece Peerless Beef Hoist company, which was about to embark on a sales campaign to send thousands of flyers—printed in Spanish—to Central and South American businesses, since raising cattle was a primary industry in those places. At that time, Elva R. Treece was head of the business, having been a part of it with her husband and continuing in the business after his death. It had been at the same location on North Main Street since it began. "Mrs. Treece, herself, can assemble several of the outfits in a day unaided," said the article. "The hoists, it is claimed, will last a lifetime. W.E. Woodward, former East Findlay butcher, claims to have purchased the first hoist made by the firm 40 years ago. It is still in use by his son and grandson."

And if that rope broke and a huge hunk of beef fell on you, at least you would have the peace of mind of knowing that the Findlay Casket Works was available not far away, just in case you didn't pull through.

"Funk & Plotner have just finished the work of erecting the Findlay Casket Works, on Cherry Street, and have secured a number of skilled workmen from Kalamazoo, Mich.," stated a report in an October 1897 edition of the *Weekly Jeffersonian*. "They expect soon to be able to put as fine caskets on the market as are made anywhere."

A mere two years later, this industry was making a killing—um, was doing quite well. Not only did the factory make "about twenty styles of cloth-covered caskets of handsome design, richly furnished with the best of cloth," according to the *Daily Courier* in early 1899, but business was so good, products were expanded to include things like "sand reels, bull wheels, cants, arms, pins, oil tanks, cisterns, and all kinds of building material, such as flooring, sash, door, blinds, siding, etc.," leading to a booming business throughout the Ohio and Indiana oil fields and even as far away as Texas, Tennessee and Virginia.

The business flourished; a notice in a 1912 *Hancock Courier* speculated about the factory's participation in a trade show: "Its products are shipped over much territory, but its managers are awake to great ramifications. A display of caskets would not mean that Findlay is dead, but on the other hand would show that the dead ones have to come here to be properly outfitted for their last resting place." The factory gave up the ghost in 1917.

AMERICAN MASK MANUFACTURING COMPANY— FINDLAY

Established in 1884 by Oscar Kirsten and Christian Heyn, both originally from Germany, the American Mask Manufacturing Company factory grew from a one-room facility to the largest (and, for a long time, the only) mask-making factory in the United States. The factory, located on West Main Cross Street, just west of the Lake Erie & Western Railroad, became so successful in such a short period of time that Kirsten asked two other families from Germany to come and help with the enterprise. His brother Otto and Otto's new bride arrived in Findlay in 1885, and Otto became a third partner in the company. As the *Findlay Weekly Republican* put it in February 1888, "It is gratifying to hear of the prosperity of such worthy and plucky young men as Messrs. Kirsten and Heyn."

Later that year, Heyn left the company and bought a half-interest in a local weekly German newspaper, the *Wochenblatt* (weekly leaf).

Purchasing Heyn's portion of the mask factory was Sebastian Baker, "one of our most substantial and enterprising citizens," according to the *Morning Republican*. The *Daily Courier* called Baker "a wealthy pioneer German citizen of Findlay, who is an untiring worker and good financier." The factory went from a workforce of three to thirty in no time.

The company's products at that time included papier mâché masks, dominoes (think Lone Ranger mask), masks of linen and wax, masks of

American Mask Manufacturing Company was located on West Main Cross Street near the Lake Erie & Western Railroad. *Courtesy of the Hancock Historical Museum.*

The staff of the American Mask Manufacturing Company, including Oscar (*back left*) and Otto (*back right*) Kirsten, posed for this 1890s photo. *Courtesy of the Hancock Historical Museum.*

comic characters of the era and noses. The company even sent a huge order of ten thousand papier mâché bucks' heads to a firm in Milwaukee in 1891.

Masks were made of moistened layers of gauze wrapped around a mold made of clay or plaster of Paris, then dried with steam heat. Faces were painted with vegetable pigment paints and then sprayed with wax to prevent running.

Politics played a role in the factory's high and low points. Of concern in the mid-1880s, for example, was the question of tariffs. Until the creation of American Mask, retailers had imported masks from Europe. Whereas European factories paid low wages for long hours, American labor was well compensated. The *Findlay Weekly Republican* opined: "An increase in the tariff duty on masks would make the American Mask Factory, in this city, one of our largest and most prosperous manufacturing establishments. It has to compete against factories in Europe that pay their employees half as much as they pay and work them fifteen or sixteen hours per day."

The mask factory also obtained some lucrative contracts thanks to politics. In 1888, the company filled an order for three thousand President Grover Cleveland caps for a firm in Columbus. In addition to many campaign orders, the factory made large "campaign masks" of Republicans Benjamin Harrison and his running mate Levi Morton, as well as Democrats Grover Cleveland and his running mate Allen G. Thurman "for use in processions."

Most campaign paraphernalia consisted of things like badges, canes, flags and fans. But an enterprising young Chicagoan, C. Boone Vastine, designed and commissioned something he felt would outperform all those mundane items: paper masks of the politicians' faces. According to an almost tongue-in-cheek article in the *Chicago Times*, which the *Hancock Courier* reprinted in September 1892, "Friends of the Democratic nominee can buy Grover Cleveland's face done in burnt sienna and ochre on a mask molded to the ex-president's features, and supplied with an elastic that holds it against the purchaser's head. Followers of Ben. Harrison can for a few brief cents procure a cast of the little man's countenance, whiskers and all, executed in rare coloring and with an attention to detail that defies the critic." Pale masks, ruddy masks, tanned masks—all were available for each candidate based on whatever the buyer wanted. The article went on to say that Vastine didn't have masks of the candidates representing the farmers' alliance and Prohibition, "but he can make them to order on short notice, and in any style or quantity desired."

Vastine, a purported distant relative of Daniel Boone, didn't want these masks to be worn on an everyday basis, "except by men who are cranks on the tariff question and given to talking." Nor should the masks be worn in bed, the article advised, unless the man's face was so ugly that it would give him nightmares.

The masks, in this young inventor's mind, were to be worn in great political processions instead of marchers simply wearing a badge or carrying a cane. "A regiment of Cleveland faces coming down the street marshaled by another Cleveland face on horseback, led by a platoon of Cleveland faces with blouse coats and stars, and interspersed with brass bands blowing out of Cleveland faces into brass horns, would be a scene of campaign splendor. And a long line of men all wearing the head of Benjamin and grandpa's hat would fill the boyish heart with glee," the *Times* continued.

Vastine turned his dream into reality by doing a little research and discovered that only one mask factory existed in the United States—the American Mask Manufacturing Company in Findlay, Ohio. "He grabbed a gripsack and an attorney, and took a train for Findlay." In a day, he had secured a contract for the company to make false faces for him—and him alone—during the presidential campaign.

American Mask agreed to supply Vastine with over seven thousand masks per day until November. Vastine would then paint them in colors preferred by the customer. He also "advertised" using men with sandwich boards and more men marching behind wearing the masks of Cleveland or Harrison. Little to no campaigning was done by either candidate, however. Harrison's wife was dying of tuberculosis (she passed away two weeks before the election), and he preferred to stay with her. Out of respect for Harrison's situation, Cleveland also did little in the way of campaigning.

During the summer of 1899, Otto Kirsten headed to the Pacific Coast to seek out new customers in Los Angeles, San Francisco, Seattle and Portland. "The company now has many retail customers along the coast, but Mr. Kirsten hopes to interest some large jobbers in his company's goods on this trip," reported the *Findlay Republican*. Products were also sent to Canada and Europe, and another large customer came in the form of Mardi Gras in New Orleans.

Although summer was considered the "dullest season of the year for business," American Mask filled orders the whole year around. And as the orders poured in, the factory itself grew, so by 1902, it had become a four-story building with a larger workforce and was still the only factory of its kind in the country. Four years later, the company was building yet another addition to its already enormous factory. This addition was built along the Lake Erie & Western Railroad switch to be used not so much for storage, since the products were shipped almost as soon as they were completed, but for ease of loading and unloading. A large door in the center of the addition provided easy access to the rail cars. "The building is covered with fluted galvanized iron, which will be painted, thus making the exterior practically fireproof," the *Courier Union* reported, as plans were announced in the newspaper.

In 1907, a natural gas well drilled on the American Mask property provided the business with more than enough fuel to run the factory. Some of the merchandise shipped that year included "four large donkeys," according to the *Courier Union*. "By this we do not mean real donkeys, for they are only imitation. They were placed in large crates, and one would think they were real to look at them and stroke their back. But they are not of the 'kicking Maud' variety. The mask factory not only makes masks but all kinds of dummy animals, from mice to elephants." Many of these shipments went to New York City.

In the summer of 1912, the Fort Findlay Centennial Celebration took place and was a showcase for Findlay businesses and industries. "By no means the least attraction of the Fort Findlay Centennial celebration is the industrial exhibit given at the headquarters of the Findlay Business Men's association and Findlay Board of Trade in the Tavern hotel block on south Main street," the *Weekly Jeffersonian* reported. From Hancock Brick & Tile to the Findlay Casket Company to the American Mask Manufacturing Company, hometown products were displayed. "The American Mask factory exhibit includes masks and false faces of all kinds and for all purposes. It also includes a papier mâché skeleton and a half of a pig, the latter the first ever made and intended as a meat market sign."

Later that year, the mask factory shipped six camels and eight horses (all canvas "dummy animals," of course) to a company in Rochester, New York.

The cover of the company's 1915 catalog, *Illustrated Catalogue of Papier Mâché, Linen, Wax, Wire, Gauze, Show and Curtain Masks* depicts some of the grotesque and unique masks and costumes available and what materials were used. The catalog's preface explains, "Thirty-one years ago we permanently established the first Mask Manufacturing Establishment in the United States of America, and having had years of experience in Europe, we feel confident we can supply the trade with superior goods, with the additional advantage of being able to ship them on short notice at all times. We guarantee low prices, and propose by fair dealing to merit a continuance of the extensive patronage we have thus far enjoyed."

In today's climate, most would be amazed—and possibly offended—by the types of masks offered to customers. Some assorted paper masks were listed as "Dutchmen, Irishmen, Indian, Clowns, Negroes, Old Men, Old Women, Jews, Chinese, Yankees, Englishmen School Boys and Girls." The catalogue also listed monks, devils, gypsies, Uncle Sam, Bedouins, Arabs, farmers, Mexicans, cowboys, tramps, hermits and police. Animal masks were also available. Masks of "Prominent Men," such as Washington, Lincoln, Taft and Roosevelt, were offered for as little as twenty-four dollars per gross. Many of the comic characters of the day were available, too, such as Happy Hooligan, Gloomy Gus, Mrs. Katzenjammer and Buster Brown. Hats, bonnets, hair, mustaches and beards could be added to almost every mask.

By 1920, the Kirsten brothers had been in business for well over thirty-five years, and Otto was ready to retire. Oscar bought out his brother and continued to run the company on his own. But Oscar Kirsten only spent a few years as president and sole owner of the company. One night, after enjoying

Workers at the American Mask Manufacturing Company made masks of devils, skulls, animals and more. *Courtesy of the Hancock Historical Museum.*

a meal at the Elks' Home, seemingly in good health and commenting on how busy he had been lately, he was playing cards when he suddenly "fell into a faint and in less than a minute's time was dead," according to the *Morning Republican* of October 16, 1926. Within ten years, Otto, too, had died "from infirmities at the age of 81." The business remained in the family, though, until the 1940s.

In 1937, when the area was celebrating the fifty-year anniversary of the discovery of gas and oil in Hancock County, the *Findlay Republican Courier* published an article about one of the city's businesses from the 1880s that was still running over fifty years later. Methods and machinery had evolved and improved throughout the years, and competition grew with the addition of a handful of other mask-making concerns, but the American Mask Manufacturing Company was still the largest business of its kind in the United States.

"The company has now extended its line of products and does an extensive business in the manufacture of masks and 'stands' for plays and many of the major masquerade celebrations of the country, as well as ether masks for hospitals, lodge regalia, papier mâché decorations and novelties," said the article. Of course, the New Orleans Mardi Gras continued to be one of the largest purchasers of the company's products, and novelties became a hit at the Toronto Fair. Ray W. Fenstermaker, secretary-treasurer of American Mask, added that the factory received what he termed "continuous surprise orders" from various celebrations around the country, and "that adds to the interest of conducting the mask manufacturing business." Fenstermaker remained general manager when Kenneth B. Champ and associates purchased the factory in 1944 following the death of Laura Kirsten, Oscar's wife.

In addition to masks, the company produced pairs of huge feet, large heads, "protruding false-stomachs for masculine disguises," a wrapped Egyptian mummy and all kinds of noses.

The company continued to prosper for some time, gaining notoriety throughout the state and country. In the 1940s, many people from Hancock County would tune into a radio show known as *The Ohio Story*. An episode in October 1948 featured the mask factory in its dramatization series. The factory even landed in a national magazine when it was featured in the October 25, 1952 issue of *Collier's*. The article, entitled "BOO!" noted that one out of six people in the United States purchase masks during the Halloween season, and the machines in Findlay's American Mask company "whip out about 1,000 masks a day," most costing between ten and twenty-five cents. "At American, for instance, they make three-headed demons, purple-phizzed oxen [whatever *that* is], whole donkeys and half-monkeys, mummies, skeletons and scores of other nightmare creatures designed to be worn, hung from ceilings or lugged around to house parties."

Other national media got into the act of reporting on the mask factory, too. In 1953, the popular television show *What's My Line?* aired an episode in October featuring Fred Elsea Jr., general manager of Findlay's American Mask Manufacturing Company. The basic premise of the show was to allow four celebrity panelists to ask yes-or-no questions of the "mystery" guest in an attempt to guess his or her occupation, or "line of work," hence the title of the program. The moderator, John Daly, would flip a card over for each "no" answer until ten cards had been flipped or the guest's "line" had been deduced.

One of the panelists the night Elsea was interviewed was Bennett Cerf, an author, publisher and punster who had actually visited Findlay as a lecturer. When he discovered that the mystery guest was from Findlay, Cerf guessed that he must be the famous playwright Russell Crouse, who hailed from Findlay. Another "no" card was flipped. Other clues that the panelists received included that a product was manufactured; it was made to be worn by men, women or children; and it was usually seasonal. Columnist Dorothy Kilgallen finally guessed correctly that Elsea worked for a mask-making firm. *Findlay Republican Courier* writer Peg Dennis finished her column "Cream for Your Morning Coffee by Peg" by pointing out that as thrilling as the experience probably was for Elsea, "the incident which topped them all came when Fred stepped on the homeward bound plane and the air stewardess said, 'Didn't I see you on television last night?'"

Although the American Mask factory closed its doors in the 1960s, masks made by this company remain in circulation. One mask was advertised on an auction site in 2012 for $265—"The Yellow Kid," or Mickey Dugan, a character in one of the first newspaper comic strips in the country. Another vintage item for sale at that time was a bear costume complete with "papier mâché bear head, hand painted and covered in brown faux fur, the faux fur suit, hands with nails of felt, and feet." A stamp reading "American Mask Manufacturing Co. Findlay, Ohio," was on the inside of the mask, and the costume was made to fit someone around five-foot-one. Another vintage mask of a man with hair coiling into a long, scraggily beard was in "good condition, but the hair needs a cleaning and careful brushing."

So, if you're in the market for a Findlay-made mask or costume, it might not be too late to acquire one. In the words of the *Daily Courier* in February 1899: "You pays your money and you takes your choice."

Glessner Medicine Company—Findlay

Sometimes, the skills gained in a job that no longer appeals to you are exactly the skills needed to break loose and begin an entirely new venture. This is (sort of) what happened to the greatly esteemed Findlay businessman Leonard "Len" Cowles Glessner, who turned a "sideline" into a nationally recognized business.

Glessner started in the newspaper business, first working for his father, Lewis, and learning the printing trade in Findlay, then at other offices throughout the Midwest, editing and publishing several papers.

Findlay's allure, however, brought him back in 1887 to become the city editor at the *Findlay Courier*, which his father had published until his death in 1879. Leonard's brother Fred had continued publishing the paper since then, keeping it all in the family, so to speak.

While at the newspaper, Len became interested in creating "remedies" from formulas he had discovered and purchased. One such formula was for a cough and croup reliever, which proved to eventually bring him fame and fortune, with a few setbacks here and there, and would bring notoriety to the city of Findlay.

His first "factory" was nothing more than his basement and attic— one room for concocting the remedy and the other for bottling it. This tonic was known as "Dr. Drake's German Cough and Croup Remedy," the formula for which Glessner had purchased from Dr. August Drake, a German physician who lived in Iowa. Glessner began replicating this recipe in the late 1880s and began labeling, bottling, packaging and selling it in 1892.

Feeling it necessary to devote more time to his new business, Glessner left the *Courier* and began the incorporation of the Drake Medicine Company in 1892. As he was no longer able to accomplish what he wanted to at his home, the new company sought a place to rent for offices and a laboratory. An August 1892 *Daily Courier* article reported: "The purpose of the company is to manufacture and sell the proprietory [*sic*] medicine known as Dr. Drake's German Croup Remedy, which is favorably known to the people of this city." Proprietary medicine (also known as patent medicine) at that time consisted of so-called remedies manufactured by private individuals or factories that may (or may not) have been patented or trademarked. "The German Croup Remedy is a well-tested medicine having been on the market for several years, and by its own merits has found its way over a large part of Northwestern Ohio. There has never

BABY IS SAFE

Dr. Drake's Glessco
Cough and Croup Remedy

A Guaranteed Remedy for Croup, Whooping Cough, Coughs, Colds, Hoarseness, Etc.

Guaranteed by The Glessner Medicine Co. under the Food and Drugs Act of June 30, 1906.—No. 70.

IN the dead of night what are you to do if the hoarse "bark" of your child awakens you, and you find him nearly strangling with the deadly Croup? Instant action may be necessary to save the child's life. Perhaps a physician can not reach you quick enough. Moments may count for the life or death of your little one. The suffocating phlegm which gathers in the throat may bring on the terrible paroxysms which come with the fight for breath. What is there that will clear the little throat? What will open up the air passages, relax the rigid muscles and bring relief?

DR. DRAKE'S GLESSCO COUGH AND CROUP REMEDY has brought relief to thousands of sufferers. Usually after ONE DOSE the heavy, labored breathing gives way to free respiration, the air passages are opened and the phlegm is dissolved. For safety's sake you may repeat the dose in fifteen or twenty minutes, and be assured that the attack is relieved. In severe cases the Croup Remedy may be given in repeated doses, until the little patient finds relief.

CROUP has been represented as one of the most terrifying of all children's diseases. It frequently comes without warning in the middle of the night, and clutches children with sudden and awful power. It has been truly called the **Terror of the Night**. It is alarming because of the suddenness of the attack, and because any child is liable to be stricken without much warning. While spasmodic croup does not usually terminate fatally, there is danger in delay, and one can not always tell this from the more dangerous membranous croup.

Dr. Drake's Glessco Cough and Croup Remedy was one of several products made and distributed by the Glessner Medicine Company. *Courtesy of the Hancock Historical Museum.*

been known a case where it has failed to cure, and it has no equal in the market." However, no resources were cited to back up this claim.

And the tonic was guaranteed, to boot! An ad that ran in the *Daily Courier* in 1895 assured the public that every bottle of Dr. Drake's German Remedy™ would "cure Croup in any of its forms" and was "the best remedy for Coughs, Colds, Hoarseness, Whooping Cough and all Diseases of the Throat and Lungs." The ad was accompanied by testimonials from men who claimed that Dr. Drake's had saved the lives of their children.

By the end of the nineteenth century, the Drake Medicine Company had become the Glessner Medicine Company and had moved to larger accommodations—the entire second floor of the Turner Opera House Building on West Main Cross Street. According to the *Daily Courier* in November 1899, "Mr. Glessner has his own mechanical and printing office and everything is prepared, made, packed and shipped from his office." Not only could he create the product and packaging, he could also print his own advertisements to be sent far and wide.

Life was good for the Glessner Medicine Company and Dr. Drake's German Croup Remedy. That is, until 1901, when Glessner found himself in common pleas court with Dr. Drake—not *the* Dr. August Drake of Iowa but a Dr. Warren Drake of Findlay. Findlay's Dr. Warren Drake apparently thought that he could capitalize on his name by creating and marketing a product with basically the same name, label and packaging. Confusion ensued. Glessner contended that Dr. Warren Drake was selling an imitation product to people who thought they were purchasing Glessner's product. According to court records, Glessner's attorney argued that the defendant, Dr. W.W. Drake, "has falsely and fraudulently given out, by speech, act and written advertisement, that he is the Dr. Drake who originated or prepared the formula used in the preparation of plaintiff's remedy hereinbefore described, when in truth and in fact the said defendant Warren W. Drake did not originate or prepare the said formula." In addition, Dr. Drake had allegedly advertised with wholesalers and druggists, leading consumers to believe that they were purchasing the "real deal" when it was strictly an imitation.

When the dust finally settled and Glessner's reputation was intact (unlike that of Dr. Warren Drake), two years had passed. The *Weekly Jeffersonian* recalled the trial of 1901 that had led to the eventual outcome in 1903. Glessner "secured a favorable verdict in the common pleas court and this verdict was affirmed by the circuit court, after which it was carried to the supreme court of Ohio, which body, on Tuesday affirmed the verdict of the lower courts making the injunction perpetual."

The roller coaster ride that was Glessner Medicine raced down a hill the following year with a fire in Findlay. Glessner's relatively new digs on the second floor of the Turner Building were almost totally ruined by a fire that was apparently caused by a defective flue. According to the *Hancock Courier* in January 1904: "Before it was discovered flames had crept in between the roof and the ceiling and were eating their way into the lathwork between the brick walls and the plastering. They burst forth and shot badly into a huge dome in the center of the building and shot up into the open air like flames from a blast furnace, when the heat became

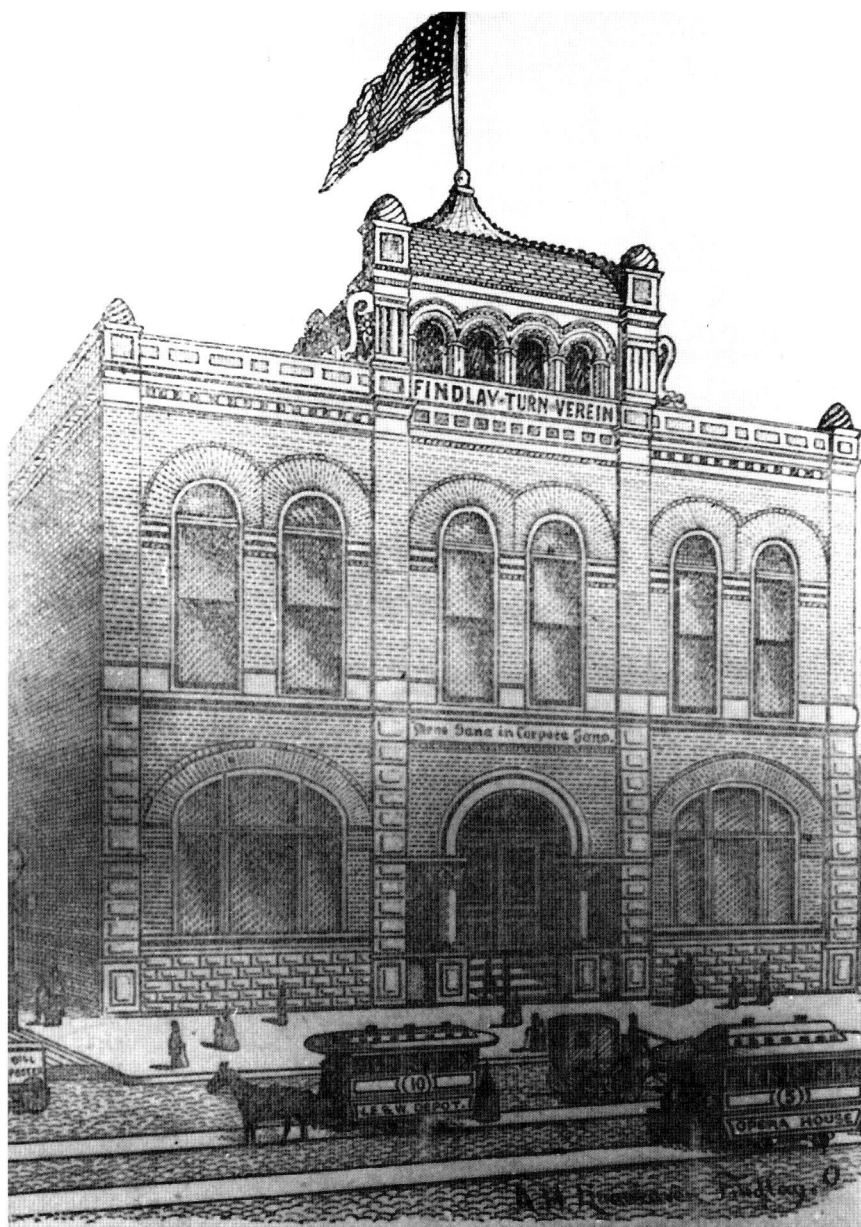

At one time, the Glessner Medicine Company maintained offices, a printing area and workspace on the second floor of the Turner Opera House building. This print was created by local doctor and artist A.H. Lineweaver. *Courtesy of the Hancock Historical Museum.*

so intense that the glass broke and fell with a crash to the floor." Glessner lost almost everything in terms of medicines, drugs and fixtures, but the printing presses sustained very little damage. As the optimistic Glessner pointed out after discovering several hundred dollars' worth of drugs and other ingredients were undamaged, "While I am a loser I did not lose as heavily as I thought I would."

The Turner Building was soon reconstructed—this time with a flat roof rather than the dome—and the Glessner Medicine Company moved what they could to temporary quarters in a building on North Main Street, with plans to begin work there on a Friday a couple of weeks after the fire. But that ol' roller coaster started slowly climbing uphill, and Findlay suffered yet another flood. Glessner and his employees were, for a time, unable to get across the Blanchard River bridge to the North Main Street Gibbs Building. Two months later, another flood caused two feet of water to flow into that building.

Despite the mishaps, the company soon incorporated, with the primary purpose of adding capital, thus allowing for more advertising in more states and, as Judge A.E. Kerns, one of the incorporators, stated, "to develop the business until every family in the United States knows of the merits of the croup remedy," adding that Glessner Medicine Company, because of the advertising, was also spreading the name of Findlay, Ohio, throughout the country.

When the Turner Building was completely refurbished, Glessner Medicine Company finally moved back to its second-floor accommodations, where it continued to operate for a few more years.

In 1911, Glessner Medicine Company invited hundreds of guests to a reception and to tour its newest quarters, a nineteenth-century Italianate structure (and former home of Judge Kerns) located at 228–234 East Sandusky Street. "The building was decorated throughout with flowers, which were the gifts of patrons and friends of the concern," reported the *Weekly Jeffersonian* in November 1911. On the tour, guests heard about and saw how the equipment worked while observing employees. "The machines used in the manufacture and mixing of the various medicines are able to turn out several thousand bottles of the product each day," stated the article in the *Jeffersonian*.

Everyone left the gala with gifts: a carnation, a sample of Dr. Drake's remedy and a folding sanitary cup. Besides Dr. Drake's German Croup Remedy, this new factory manufactured Leonard's Sweet Worm Wafers, with its ads proclaiming: "A positive cure for Worms, Feverishness, Constipation and other disorders of children. Pleasant as candy, harmless, ready for use. Sold by all druggists 25c per box."

In a few years, Glessner Medicine Company took on a new name and began manufacturing a new product. The March 1916 *Weekly Jeffersonian* announced that the company had changed its name to Glessner Company, "as a convenience in a large advertising campaign which the company is starting." The new campaign came about because of the creation of their new turpentine ointment, "Turpo."

Turpentine was the primary ingredient in this salve advertised as a cure-all for ailments such as the flu and the common cold. It could also be used on "open sores, cuts, scratches, bruises, scalds and abrasions of the skin." The advertisement noted that turpentine "has long been recognized as one of the most efficient remedies for inflammation, congestion, soreness, stiffness, cold in head or chest, sore throat, croup, tonsillitis, headache, earache, neuralgia…sunburn, chapped hands, pimples, insect bites, poison ivy, sore joints or muscles, sprains, lame back, pleurisy and lumbago."

Another advertisement in the *Hancock Herald* in 1919 claimed that President Wilson, who had apparently been suffering from exhaustion and neurasthenia following a bout with influenza the previous spring, might have warded off the nasty germs by applying a little Turpo into his nostrils. But, "remember that Turpo is a preventive, not a cure for influenza," the ad clarified.

The following year, the factory expanded once again, adding two more stories to the two-story building on East Sandusky Street and a warehouse that would face East Crawford Street. The company also reorganized to gain additional capital.

During the early twentieth century, the patent drug industry felt the ire of the medical field. An article in the October 7, 1905 issue of *Collier's Magazine* denounced patent medicine methods as being "founded on fraud and poison." This article, and many of the medical journals of the time, claimed that there were no effective laws regulating who could make a medicine— anyone could, even without a medical degree—and the ingredients that were used did not have to be divulged on a label. Millions of people, they maintained, were being duped by the promise of a cure when all they were receiving for their hard-earned money was something that might make them feel better for a short time or cause an addiction or early death, because most potions were laced with opiates, narcotics and/or alcohol.

When research showed that many of the remedies contained drugs like alcohol, opium and its derivatives (notably morphine, codeine and heroin) and cocaine, legislators took notice and passed the 1906 Pure Food and Drug Act, which stated that ingredients and their amounts had to be listed on labels. An article in a congressional edition of "Reports of the President's Homes Commission," told of "medicinal preparations" that contained "habit-forming drugs other than alcohol." Thirty-eight different remedies were listed. For example, opium could be found in Dr. Drake's German Croup Remedy and Dr. Moffett's Teething Powders, and morphine in Petit's Eye Salve, Children's Comfort and the Infant's Friend. The act did not do away with patent medicine makers and sellers, but it did make them accountable for letting the public know the makeup of each of their products.

Glessner products such as Glessco (formerly called Dr. Drake's German Croup Remedy), however, were trademarked and registered with the U.S. Patent Office. Glessco's patent, filed in January 1913, included a label listing the ingredients. A two-fluid-ounce bottle of Dr. Drake's Glessco for children contained 2.25 percent alcohol in addition to the active ingredients of ipecac and castor oil "in a vehicle containing Benzoic Acid, Gum Arabic, Camphor, Wild Cherry, Glycerine, Anise Oil, Sweetened and emulsified." The adult version contained 5 percent alcohol, along with other ingredients like ammonia, menthol, glycerin and sodium benzyl succinate.

By 1926, the Glessner Company employed thirty-five workers and was mailing eighteen million advertising flyers per year throughout the United States. Glessco and Turpo both continued to sell quite well, with 850,000 bottles of Glessco and 600,000 jars of Turpo being made during fiscal year 1925. "A company official pointed out that more Glessco is sold than all other croup remedies put together, and that Turpo ranks fourth among salves for colds," reported the *Morning Republican* in May of that year.

According to the article, Glessner "attributes the success of the company to extensive advertising, and does not believe their cold and croup remedies are selling because of more sickness." That, in a nutshell, is what critics of "patent medicine" had been complaining about for decades—the power of suggestion that a product will "cure" the patient, whether really ill or not, is more powerful than whatever that "cure" is made of.

As production and products grew, so did the factory. For two years, the company had been working on a new product and waiting to find the appropriate market for it. Harry Glessner, Leonard's son, created it and had been testing this product for eight months before the company was ready to unveil—drum roll, please—KEEN Shaving Kreem in 1927. According to an article in the *Morning Republican*, "The cream is the only one on the market

Employees at the Glessner Medicine Company appreciated the clean working conditions. *Courtesy of the Hancock Historical Museum.*

which bears a guarantee of its manufacturers." In addition, "A leading barber in Findlay yesterday began using the local product exclusively." Naturally, the company was planning "an extensive advertising campaign" to launch the shaving cream.

Remember Turpo, the turpentine ointment for colds? Well, no longer would you have to "snuff it up your nostril" for relief. Glessner Company had invented and patented the Turpo Electric Vaporizer, "as simple as plugging in a light cord in your electrical fixture." And you could get both the vaporizer (valued at one dollar and fifty cents) and a jar of Turpo (valued at seventy-five cents) for the unbelievably low price of ninety-five cents! The new device was "designed to bring relief to cold sufferers, penetrating the congestion of the most malignant cold" by using a mixture of Turpo and water in an electric appliance. Even before it had been formally introduced to the buying public, orders began streaming in. The formal introduction came in the form of a full-page ad "in all of the Magazine sections of the Sunday editions of the Hearst papers, which will be taken into more than six million homes. Incidentally Findlay as a community will receive widespread publicity."

The Turpo vaporizer became a huge success, with the company shipping over 16,000 by direct mail in January 1930—a new sales record for the company. "The postage alone on this direct mail distribution for the month of January amounted to almost $5,000." Over 500,000 vaporizers were sold in three months.

Sofskin, a lotion, was added as a product in 1936. Not only did it smell better than the cough medicine and ointment, it also found a tremendous following in the beauty salons of the day. Glessner furnished establishments with sample-size jars of Sofskin at manicure tables and regular-size jars in attractive wrappings during the Christmas and Easter seasons. Before long, the small jars became the business owners' Christmas gifts to their customers, with almost two million jars having been sold. Soon, the fragrant hand cream could be purchased at drugstores, where it became the second-largest seller in the field. Sofskin remained a Glessner product until it was sold to the Vick Chemical Company in 1946.

Another product, Pain-A-Lay, was introduced as a "Dentist's Formula Pain Relieving Antiseptic Anodyne" for sore gums "due to false teeth irritations or following teeth extractions" and sore throats "due to colds and excessive smoking." Active ingredients in Pain-A-Lay were boric acid and cresol. The formula came from three Kansas City brothers who were dentists, and the product became widely used.

Former Findlay resident Doug Smith, whose father worked for Glessner from 1948 to 1963, remembered visiting the factory on Saturdays with his brother when they were both young boys. They watched the workers fill bottles, apply labels, pack and check to make sure lids were screwed on tight and straight. He also recalled having to take Dr. Drake's and Glessco. "It tasted terrible," he remarked. Today, he has an unopened bottle of Dr. Drake's from 1963—and he has no plans to open it.

Leonard Glessner, original owner and president of the company, was active in community and business affairs well into his eighties. Besides presiding over the Glessner Company, he was an active member of the Elks and Rotary Clubs and the Findlay Country Club. As he was walking to his home on South Main Street from a dinner meeting at the Elks' Home on a November evening in 1936, he was struck by a young driver who did not see him as he was crossing the street. She stopped the car, engine still running, and hurried to the nearest house to call for an ambulance. Unfortunately, the eighty-three-year-old Glessner never regained consciousness, and he died the following day.

Ironically, a similar fate befell his brother Fred the following month as he was crossing Main Street on his way to a restaurant for breakfast. He was ninety years old.

The Glessner Company continued to be successful and profitable under the able management of Leonard's son Harry, who became president when his father died, and Leonard's daughter Mary, the treasurer. The business continued until 1962, when it was sold to the Denver Chemical Manufacturing Company of Stamford, Connecticut. Even after that sale, the Glessner Company name remained on its products.

4

SKIVVIES TO STOGIES

G irls Wanted," "Ladies Wanted," "Extra Pay for Girls," "We Want Havana Strippers"—this isn't what you are probably thinking. These were some of the newspaper want ads advertising and competing for female employees at three Findlay factories during the early part of the twentieth century. The C.C. Anderson Underwear Manufacturing Company, the Boss Glove Manufacturing Company and the Deisel-Wemmer Cigar Factory all hired many more women than they did men.

C.C. Anderson Underwear Manufacturing Company

The Findlay facility of the C.C. Anderson Underwear Manufacturing Company opened in 1905, occupying the entire third floor of a large building at the corner of Howard and North Main Streets. Specializing in women's muslin and flannelette undergarments, this factory employed around fifty people—mostly girls—when it started and produced about forty-five cases of merchandise per day. Business was so good during its first year that the company more than doubled its workforce, enlarged the building, increased the amount of floor space and purchased additional sewing machines.

In the beginning, the third floor housed a cutting room, a workroom, stockrooms and a shipping area. Garments were first cut out and then sent to the workroom, where the pieces were sewn together. Finally, the underwear was packaged and ready to ship throughout the country. Average wages ranged from $1.10 to $2.50 per day.

The Findlay location was a branch of the Fostoria-based underwear company; both factories were working at capacity and, at times, had to turn down some of the many requested orders. The Findlay plant needed more workers and could not understand why so few women were applying for jobs. It turned out that many women read the "Girls Wanted" advertisements and assumed that it meant nothing but young girls, when, in fact, women of all ages were being sought. In 1907, the ad was changed to "Ladies Wanted," and employment applications increased.

The following year, the Anderson Underwear Manufacturing Company filled all three floors of the Findlay building. The first floor included a shipping area and a new retail store to sell merchandise made in the factory. Part of the second floor was office space, and part was factory space. The third floor continued to be used as a factory. About one hundred women and girls were employed at that time, and because of additional orders, the entire workforce labored every day and for three evenings each week.

The building where the C.C. Anderson Underwear Manufacturing Company had its factory still stands at the corner of North Main and Howard Streets. *Courtesy of the author.*

The Ohio Muslin Underwear Company located in Findlay after the C.C. Anderson Underwear Manufacturing Company left the area. *Courtesy of the Hancock Historical Museum.*

In the early 1910s, rumor had it that the underwear factory would soon be under new management. According to a March 1910 *Republican Jeffersonian* article, "Owing to mismanagement and the excessively high salaries, the entire plant was thrown into bankruptcy recently and bought in at public sale by a class of men who are familiar with the business and expect, in a short time, to place the plant on a paying basis." However, the promise of a new industry at the corner of Howard and Main Streets disintegrated when Fostoria Blue Bow Undermuslin Company, the intended buyers, closed, and the company representative was instructed to sell the Findlay building.

BOSS GLOVE MANUFACTURING COMPANY

The Boss Glove Manufacturing Company, which originated in Kankakee, Illinois, in 1893, soon placed several branch factories around the Midwest. In 1903, the company bought the Houck Brothers Glove Manufactory on Liberty Street in Findlay, retaining the Houck brothers as part of the new business venture—this was a smart move on everyone's part.

What had begun as a small one-room factory with around fifty employees grew into a vastly successful business with several hundred employees working at an enormous three-story factory producing cloth work gloves and mittens.

In 1906, a *Courier Union* reporter toured the expanded facility. General manager William E. Houck acted as guide. Houck's private office, the reporter observed, "is fitted up with all of the modern conveniences."

The engine room, located behind the office, contained "two twenty-five horse power gas engines, and a three hundred light dynamo, the private property of the company and affords illumination for the entire building." Another room held two machines and a cutting table that could hold six hundred yards (spread out) of fabric. Parts of gloves were cut using a die and then sent to the sewing rooms, where each person had a specific job in joining the parts together. At that time, 125 girls ran the sewing machines, while other employees sorted and packed the gloves for shipping:

> *All gloves and mittens are sewed wrong side out, and from the sewing department they go to the turning department. In this department every glove and mitten is drawn over a metal form, carefully examined, seams smoothed down, etc., after which they are sorted in pairs, in stacks of a dozen each and bound in a carton with the stock number on the same. The different departments of the factory are connected by local telephone. The gloves are used by men and women for all classes of work.*

The factory accommodated the employees with a dining area, restroom facilities, a place to lie down if not ill enough to lose a day's pay by leaving work and other amenities. "The entire building is well lighted and ventilated and judging from the general appearance of the girls, their neat dresses and cleanliness, they enjoy their work and are prosperous."

In March 1907, Boss Glove planned to open a branch in Bluffton and had Bluffton girls come to Findlay's plant to learn the trade. The *Republican Jeffersonian* reported that "it will employ thirty girls and about a dozen men at the start, while as the factory continues in operation, more will be brought into service." The company had ordered twenty-six sewing machines. The plant would be located in the Mitsch Block on Bluffton's North Main Street, using the first floor of the building for the sewing machines and the second floor for storage.

Six months later, an article in the *Hancock Courier* questioned why not enough young ladies were available for hire at the Bluffton glove plant, deducing that the big cigar factories of Lima and surrounding places were luring the girls away with better wages. The people of Bluffton considered the factory "almost a necessity and they will be loath to part with it. It is stated, however, that a location will in all probability be sought right here

Boss Glove Factory, Findlay, Ohio.

The Boss Glove Manufacturing Company was located on West Main Cross and Liberty Streets. *Courtesy of the Hancock Historical Museum.*

in Hancock county where there are many small towns just running over with girls. Among these under consideration are: Arlington, McComb, Mt. Blanchard or Rawson." Spoiler alert: Bluffton's Boss Glove factory lasted nearly fifty years before closing in November 1956.

The Findlay plant continued to expand. In 1910, over 450 people, mostly women, worked at the glove factory, and contracts for $25,000 worth of improvements were awarded to construct a new three-story building and an addition to the existing building, extending it to West Main Cross Street. The structures would be connected by passageways on all three floors.

To retain the female employees of Boss Glove, the company made a new rule in 1913 stating that girls would be granted a bonus of ten percent if they didn't lose any time. If an employee earned six dollars per week and was at work for the full number of hours, she would receive an additional sixty cents in her pay envelope. With the girls in demand at other plants in Findlay, this incentive worked to keep them at Boss Glove.

Five years later, the average weekly output at this plant ranged from 12,000 to 15,000 dozen pairs of gloves per day. That's 288,000 to 360,000 gloves—every week. Each of the three hundred girls at the three hundred sewing machines would make between twenty-five and thirty gloves per day, every day.

Finished gloves were packed in fourteen-foot-high bins in an 8,600-square-foot storeroom, waiting to be shipped. The busiest shipping months were July through November.

William E. Houck, who retired in 1947 after forty-four years as manager of the Boss Manufacturing Company, contributed much more to Findlay and Hancock County than merely running a successful factory. A civic-minded man, he also was instrumental in starting the local Rotary Club in 1920, and he organized the chamber of commerce in Findlay. His interests and activities included the YMCA, baseball (he had pitched for a Findlay club in the 1890s), Findlay College (his alma mater) and several fraternal organizations. Following his retirement from Boss Glove, he became president of the Hancock Savings and Loan Company. But perhaps one of his greatest achievements was turning a small glove-making business into one of the largest in the country through his dedication and determination.

Today, the Boss Glove building, next to the Great Scot Community Market, houses offices for Fresh Encounter, Inc. *Courtesy of the author.*

In December 1961, Boss Manufacturing announced that due to fewer experienced sewing employees at the plant (forty-five, compared to hundreds in years past), the Findlay plant would be closing. The representative from the headquarters in Kankakee assured workers who wanted to continue employment with the company that they could find work at any of the seven other Boss plants located in Illinois, Texas and Missouri. He regretted having to close the plant, which would then be used as a warehouse, with about five employees, but he said it was a matter of economics.

CIGAR FACTORIES

Black Duck, Juno, SS, Zobo, San Felice and El Verso—smoke 'em if you got 'em!

During the gas and oil boom days in the 1880s, Findlay was home to at least five cigar factories, which, in a few years, grew to ten. Most were small family-operated "factories" in homes or shops that had only a few employees.

In 1899, the *Daily Courier* reported on the cigar industry: "It has been estimated that from two to three million cigars and stogies are made annually in Findlay." Not only were cigars being made in Findlay, but at one time, tobacco for the cigar manufacturers was being grown in Hancock County.

In 1906, cigar manufacturer George Neymeyer, who had also held the position of mayor of Findlay, launched a "new enterprise, which bids fair to reach stupendous proportions and be an excellent source of revenue to the farmers of the community." Neymeyer felt Hancock County soil would successfully raise tobacco and offered seeds to interested farmers willing to plant an acre or two, adding more land and farmers in the subsequent years. "It should not be any more of a trick to raise tobacco in Ohio and around here than any other place," added the article.

And then…chickens. Neymeyer and his family were out of town one day and came home to a disaster. According to an article in a June 1908 *Republican Jeffersonian*, he had a "hot bed of fine plants near his residence, containing several thousand grown from the choicest seed, furnished him by Prof. Selby, of the State Experiment Station at Wooster. He sowed the seed on the 15th of March, and the plants were nearly a foot high. He had taken three or four hundred plants from the bed and replanted them in a field, and intended replanting the remaining thousands in a day or two." While he was away, chickens from a neighboring farm visited his tobacco hotbed and "didn't cease until nearly every plant was scratched out and lay dead in the sun on the return of the family." About a hundred plants were saved, but it was too late in the year to plant more for the next season.

Other entrepreneurs preferred to raise their tobacco in Florida. The SS cigar factory, located on Meeks Avenue (since 1893), and the Zobo factory on Cherry Street (since 1890) sent representatives to Florida in 1906 to research the soil and purchase a farm for growing tobacco. They found a tract bordered by the Georgia, Florida & Alabama and Sea Board Air Line Railroads with a small navigable river nearby. Mules were used for the farm work "because horses cannot stand the heat." A large building served as a place to sort, shade, cure, bale and prepare the tobacco for shipment to Findlay.

Another company, Juno Cigar, moved from the McKelvey Block on South Main Street to a shop at 211 South Main Street and operated a store used for both retail and wholesale business. "The big dog, Juno, still sits in the window holding the [advertising] card and seems as much at home as in the old room in the McKelvey block," stated a comment in the *Courier Union* in 1907.

DEISEL-WEMMER CIGAR COMPANY

However, 1910 was the year that changed the cigar industry in Findlay. The Deisel-Wemmer Cigar Company of Lima proposed locating a branch in Findlay. At that time, the company had six branches but was still having trouble keeping up with orders. The fourth floor of the Rawson Building in downtown Findlay became their seventh branch.

In 1912, while a new, four-story building with a basement was being constructed on Broadway Street, the Rawson Building workers continued to manufacture San Felice cigars. Two hundred employees—men, women, and boys—made and shipped 150,000 cigars each week.

The basement of the new factory held the heating plant and served as a huge storage room. The first floor contained offices and shipping and stripping departments. A dining area, bathrooms, and a space for workers to "promenade during their lunch hour" filled the second floor. The cigars were manufactured on the third floor, and the packing and drying rooms were on the fourth, with overhead lights and a skylight so the tobacco could receive an even amount of northern sunlight for shading.

The Deisel-Wemmer cigar factory was located on Broadway Street in Findlay. *Courtesy of the Hancock Historical Museum.*

Just as the underwear and glove factories hired women and girls, so did the Deisel-Wemmer Cigar factory. According to a January 1913 *Hancock Courier* article,

> *the demand for girls and women in the factories has practically killed the servant girl question in Findlay. It is now next to impossible to get a girl to work in the kitchen. She can get better wages in a factory and has more time for herself. She is not at the beck and call of milady of the front room and escapes a great deal of drudgery for little pay. The servant girl problem has become quite serious in families where wealth and lack of knowing how to cook and do housework make it absolutely necessary that help be had, and just what solution of the puzzle can be made remains to be seen.*

The following year, the company announced that it would produce eleven million cigars—the largest output in its four-year history in Findlay. The

Employees of the Deisel-Wemmer cigar factory in Findlay helped produce millions of cigars. *Courtesy of the Hancock Historical Museum.*

workforce of three hundred turned out approximately fifty thousand cigars a day, all made by hand. The average pay in 1916 was between fifteen and sixteen dollars per week, and finding girls to work at the factory still proved difficult. Maybe they were all cleaning and cooking for "milady."

Productivity and wages continued to rise. The goal for 1917 was twelve million cigars. Beginning wages were set at six dollars per week, with the possibility of earning eighteen to twenty dollars per week as workers became more skilled. In 1919, the Deisel-Wemmer company managed seventeen branches and offered all of the 4,500 employees a 10 percent raise. That year, the Findlay company presented gifts of cigars and candy to the county infirmary and candy to the Children's Home.

By 1921, all cigars were made by machine, and the company added a night shift in 1922, continuing its search for female employees. An ad in the *Morning Republican* in September 1922 read: "STRIPPERS WANTED for day or evening shift. Experience not necessary." Stripping consisted of removing the center vein out of the large tobacco leaves that would be used as wrappers. Other permanent positions included packing, banding machine work and package stamping. That year, the Findlay branch produced sixteen million cigars, both San Felice and El Verso.

San Felice cigars were some of the most popular cigars made at the Findlay Deisel-Wemmer plant. This cigar box was made after the main office moved from Lima to Detroit. *Courtesy of the Hancock Historical Museum.*

In 1923, the still-growing Deisel-Wemmer company constructed a four-story addition to the rear of the existing factory, extending it to Cory Street. The Findlay plant became the second-largest cigar factory in the Deisel-Wemmer system.

In 1926, the plant was still running two shifts to meet the demand of requested orders. At that time, the day shift produced 100,000 cigars, and the night shift produced 15,000. The day shift ran from 6:30 a.m. to 5:00 p.m., and the night shift was from 4:00 p.m. to 10:00 p.m. According to the *Morning Republican*, "Many of the women favor the night shift because they are able to finish their housework in the morning and early afternoon hours, before time to work."

The company continued to grow and prosper. In 1929, Deisel-Wemmer formed a corporation, and the company became Deisel-Wemmer-Gilbert (shortened to DWG). A 1938 *Republican Courier* article described the production at DWG:

> *Here a force of 360 workers, mostly girls and women, take the tobacco in its crude leaf form, blend it so the flavor will be right, and put it through intricate machinery to turn out thousands of boxes of full-sized cigars daily, each one an almost exact counterpart of the others in color, shape,*

length, weight and flavor. The only possible exception to the rule is slight variation in color which means nothing in quality. This is taken care of by a group of skilled women workers who grade as to shade so that all cigars in the same box are the same color.

Tobacco for the Findlay plant came from Sumatra, the Dutch East Indies, Connecticut, Pennsylvania and Darke County, Ohio. The tobacco went through many stages—sampling, curing, stem removal, drying—that all occurred before it arrived in Findlay to be made into cigars:

Actually assembling the cigars is the next process and this work is carried on by 28 intricate machines which are better than human in their accuracy. Four women workers are assigned to each. One feeds the filler into the maw of the machine where automatic fingers divide it into the right portions and get it in shape of the binders. Another woman spreads a piece of binder leaf which is then automatically cut to the right size, picked up by an automatic arm and wrapped about the filler. At the same time another arm is picking up a wrapper leaf spread by another operator which also is mechanically wrapped about the filler and binder. Finally assembled, the finished cigar goes to a fourth member of the crew who examines the cigar for imperfections and either turns it back for repairs or discards it.

Inspectors weighed, measured and gauged the cigars before sending them to the packing room, where they were inspected and graded to wrapper shades. Another machine then added foil and a band before wrapping the cigar in cellophane. From there, the cigars were packed in boxes that held five to fifty cigars. Ninety-nine percent of the cigars that traveled through all of the machinery came out "as first grade and full sized," proving that the workers knew what they were doing.

Over the years, the Findlay DWG plant produced San Felice Original, San Felice King Size, Y.B. Squire, Emerson, Odin and El Verso Junior cigars—the plant made over sixty-two million cigars in 1961 alone. After the plant closed in 1962, the company was moved to Lima.

PART 3: WOODEN IT BE NICE?—LUMBER AND FURNITURE

1

LUMBERING ALONG

During the late 1700s, European settlers began forging their way into what would soon become Hancock County. At that time, it is estimated that 95 percent of this territory was forested. Robert C. Brown describes this area at the time: "It was, excepting the marsh lands, one vast, unbroken forest. The soil was deep and fertile, and bore up an abundant growth of vegetation, while the trees stood close and were of gigantic size." Many types of trees grew here, including oak, elm, ash, hickory and, of course, the buckeye for which the state is nicknamed. The pioneers saw the value in the lumber and knew that the soil beneath the forests would be advantageous for farming ventures. Therefore, little by little, the giant walnut and poplar trees that had once covered the land were felled to create houses and their stumps were removed in order for people to grow crops. Around one hundred years later, forests covered only about 10 percent of the countryside.

From the mid- to late 1800s, many of the communities in Hancock County housed factories that produced barrel staves and hoops, as well as handles for tools. From the tiny communities of Arcadia, Cory, Rawson and Shawtown to the villages of Arlington and McComb to the bustling city of Findlay, one could find factories and mills receiving logs to cut, plane and turn into necessary implements.

By 1873, the hamlets of Arcadia, in Washington Township, and Cory and Rawson, in Union Township, had manufacturing interests not only in sawmills or flouring mills but also in handle factories. In fact, Arcadia had three handle factories. Having been built along the Lake Erie & Western

Railroad through Hancock County, these three little bergs were able to be quite self-sufficient.

The village of Shawtown in Pleasant Township was laid out in June 1882, on the New York, Chicago & St Louis Railroad a few miles west of McComb but had had a post office established there the previous year. In December 1881, the *Hancock Courier* reported: "T.W. Kelley has moved to Shawtown and expects to end his days there in business where he first started several years ago. He is building a fine residence, and is one of the firms that is building a large hoop factory in said village." By the end of that decade, the businesses in the community consisted of a sawmill and hoop factory, two general stores and a blacksmith and wagon shop. The post office existed until 1923.

One Sunday in October 1884, in Arlington, the sawmill and hoop factory owned by J.M.K. Long & Company burned to the ground. The *Weekly Jeffersonian* stated: "Everything is a total loss. No insurance. The fire originated from a spark it is supposed, as the factory had been running on Saturday. We trust the community will contribute to build them up again, as this was the only property the company owned and they are broke."

Often, young boys were hired to work in the mills. One headline from the *Daily Courier* in May 1899 read, "A Little Row at the Arlington Hoop Factory Costs a Boy $2.50." Apparently, two lads were working at the factory when one of them, Johnnie Hindall, amassed a pile of shavings at his feet. He kicked the pile to get them out of his way, inadvertently knocking them into coworker Merle Stine's way. Stine, quick to anger, grabbed a wooden club and bashed Hindall in the hip, causing him to limp off to his home. A doctor examined him and declared that no bones had been broken, although the boy was badly bruised. The article concludes with, "Stine was arrested and taken before the mayor, who fined him $2.50. Boys should not let their angry passions rise. All should dwell together in loving kindness and unity."

A new building for the Arlington hoop factory was begun in 1905. J.M. Peel and Brother Company owned and operated it. The hoops were constructed from logs from area elm trees. As a worker at that factory, Rupert M. Hindall reminisced about his time at the Hoop Mill in *The Village of Arlington, 1834–1984*. He explained that the logs "were cut into lengths of about seven feet and then sawed into planks of about one and one-half inches thick. The planks then were placed in tanks of hot water and boiled, after which the plank was placed on a machine that sliced hoops off the edge of the plank."

Hindall's job as a planer involved running sliced hoops through a machine that would ensure they were smooth on the side that "was turned out when attached to the barrel." After that, the hoops went through a "lapper" to be pointed and cut so that they could be easily coiled. Hindall's wages as a planer in 1908 amounted to fifteen cents an hour. Working ten-hour days, he brought home nine dollars each week.

Several years later, in January 1913, the Peel brothers hosted a banquet and smoker for the forty workers of the hoop factory, noting that the Arlington factory was one of the largest in the state, with a daily output of sixty thousand hoops. Even so, a month later, the mill had shut down "on account of the roads being so bad that logs could not be hauled." By 1917, elm logs were becoming so scarce that the owners moved their mill to Arkansas.

In 1881, McComb was another growing community making many improvements. Thirty new buildings were to be erected, not counting the depot and engine house for the railroad. And near the depot, Frank Van Dyke built a hoop factory and sawmill.

The larger community of Findlay had at least two hoop or stave factories. The Findlay Stave and Handle Factory on West Sandusky Street became a leading manufacturer in the 1870s. According to R.C. Brown, "Staves and all kinds of farm-tool handles are the product of this factory, whose markets extend to nearly every part of the globe. Twenty-five hands are usually employed throughout the year, and the sales amount to $30,000 per annum." Another handle factory was located on Lima Road and began operations in 1881. In the spring of 1882, James P. Kerr started the Findlay Hoop Works on East Sandusky Street. He bought much of the machinery from the Findlay Carriage Bent Works, taking them to his new facility, where he employed eight men who manufactured hoops and hardwood lumber.

Not wanting to be outdone by neighboring communities, the little village of Williamstown reported in the *Findlay Weekly Union* in April 1891 that "there was a gentleman here last week hunting a location for a hoop factory. Look out Findlay; the boom is coming here." However, there is no indication that a hoop factory was, in fact, built there.

Of course, along with these smaller wood businesses, larger lumberyards came into their own.

F.S. Pendleton Lumber Company—McComb

Like many other Hancock County communities during the mid-nineteenth century, McComb had high hopes of eventually having a railroad running through it to provide transportation for travelers and allow for easier shipment of goods.

Robert C. Brown, in his *History of Hancock County*, wrote that the McComb, Deshler & Toledo Railroad Company, incorporated on June 2, 1879, came about thanks to citizens from McComb and a capital investment of $20,000 for building a railroad to connect McComb with Deshler, located about ten miles northwest in Henry County.

> *Grading was commenced in the spring of 1880, and on the 24ᵗʰ of November, following, the first construction train came into McComb. On the next day* [Thanksgiving] *the event was celebrated at McComb by a grand dinner and a flow of oratory, a large delegation coming over the road from Deshler, and a few from Findlay to participate in the happy festivities, more than 1,000 outsiders being present on the occasion.*

The following year, work was finished on the New York, Chicago & St. Louis Railway lines, which connected Fostoria, Arcadia, Stuartville, McComb and Shawtown in Hancock County. Better known as the Nickel Plate, it was "one of the leading trunk lines of the country, and supplies the north part of the county with excellent railroad accommodations," according to Brown.

Just north of the McComb, Deshler & Toledo tracks were several irregularly shaped lots that seemed, to Almon L. Hayes and Albert A. Starr, to be perfect for a lumberyard. They operated a lumber manufacturing business there until Starr sold his part of the business in 1890. The lots between the McComb, Deshler & Toledo tracks and the Nickel Plate tracks had several different owners who operated the lumberyard over the next several years until Marion V. Pendleton bought the business on December 27, 1898.

Lois Biere Pendleton, the wife of Marion's son Floyd S. Pendleton, who both owned and operated the lumber company later in the twentieth century, related some of her memories in McComb's sesquicentennial book published in 1981.

Before Marion V. Pendleton bought the business, it had been McComb Bending Company, "making bows for buggy tops and maybe some other bent articles." Although the bending company was no longer in business,

Lois Pendleton's future husband, Floyd, as a young boy, found that some remaining pieces "made good hockey sticks for the fun and games on ice." The lumberyard in the late nineteenth century not only included a sawmill but was able to turn out just about anything one would need for building a house: siding, doors, blinds and millwork. Shingles, however, were shipped in from Michigan.

Marion V. Pendleton operated the sawmill and lumberyard until late 1914, when he and another lumberyard owner in McComb sold out to the Toledo-based Robert Hixon Lumber Company, which then owned eleven lumberyards in Ohio. Both lumberyard owners maintained some interest in the new company. One condition of the sale was that Pendleton promised not to work in the lumber business (except for the sawmill) for ten years.

According to the *Hancock County Herald* of December 14, 1914, "Both of the above firms were pioneer industries of McComb. Stoker Bros. established their business in January 1896, while the Pendleton yard has been under the management of M.V. Pendleton since the purchase from O.E. Townsend, about sixteen years ago." Stoker's stock was moved to Pendleton's yard, and the machinery of both businesses was transferred elsewhere.

Pendleton was able to keep the sawmill aspect of the business—the part that he especially liked. Operating without an office for a couple of years, he was finally able to purchase a lot with a small house in 1916, and he used the house as an office. His son Floyd joined the business as an engineer who was also involved in the bookkeeping "and other things M.V. Pendleton didn't like and they operated happily together," wrote Lois.

When Floyd returned from serving in World War I, he continued to work with his father. But things had changed as far as the Hixon business was concerned. Floyd felt that the customers were being treated unfairly and without regard. In one instance, a farmer bought a load of posts and needed help reloading and tying them onto his vehicle to transport them back to his farm. Floyd, noting the price paid by the farmer, felt that the profit margin was much higher than it should have been, so he decided he could still make a profit but also ease the burden to the customer by buying carloads of posts and selling them at a more reasonable price. Since it had only been eight years, rather than ten, that M.V. Pendleton had been out of the lumber business, he couldn't, in good conscience, participate in this enterprise with Floyd.

Floyd Pendleton, with the good wishes of his father and a place to stack the posts in back of the small office building, began buying carload after carload of posts. Most of his customers were farmers and appreciated the opportunity to buy the posts at a good price. But, as Lois Pendleton noted, "Of course he was long on enthusiasm and short on capital." Between the two of them, though, they used his state bonus and her war savings and entered into a partnership.

Thanks to a little help from Marion, Floyd and Lois were able to obtain a loan—enough money to erect a small building for a car or two of lumber. It was connected to the small office building that they and Marion Pendleton would share, as Floyd would continue keeping the books for his dad.

Small ideas grew into larger ideas, and before they knew it, they added onto the building, bought another hand truck and hired Ersal Martin to help them with what needed to be done. "He was a good mechanic and learned to be a fine woodworker," wrote Lois Pendleton. "He stayed with us until his death in April 1940."

By 1922, Lois, a partner in every sense of the word, had learned a great deal about the business, including bookkeeping, typing and figuring board feet "without the use of an adding machine." Although few women at that time worked outside the home or farm, she had worked in her father's grocery store and had grown up with the attitude, supported by her father, that "girls could do anything there was to be done as well as any boy and maybe a little better." However, she found, at times, that many men did not necessarily agree with that philosophy, especially if she happened to be on her own in the lumber business office. "I found that our customers would accept me—sometimes reluctantly—if I were alone in the office but tended to ignore me if there was a man around!"

Three years later, Lois and Floyd felt that they were in a position to buy out the Hixon yard. "We made them a fair offer which they accepted," she said. "They were nice to us throughout the transaction and helpful in setting up some more adequate bookkeeping."

The *Hancock County Herald* reported on May 15, 1925, that "a deal was closed last week whereby Floyd S. Pendleton becomes owner of the Hixon holdings and the same will be consolidated with Mr. Pendleton's lumber business. The new owner is now in possession of all buildings, land and stock."

The Pendleton family continued to grow both commercially and personally. The company bought more lots and built another shop to accommodate their manufacturing expansion. It added lumberyards in Leipsic, Hoytville and Weston. And Lois discovered that she was pregnant "just as I was beginning to think I was becoming a fairly good lumberman."

The F.S. Pendleton Lumber Company in McComb was owned and operated by Floyd and Lois Pendleton for over fifty years. *Courtesy of the Hancock Historical Museum.*

She says she retired as much as she could after the birth of their daughter Leah Nell but still helped out in the business, especially during inventory time and tax season or when experienced help was required in the office. After their daughter left home for college, though, she went back to the business as a "full timer."

One of the many areas that F.S. Pendleton Lumber Company engaged in was designing and building what they called "beet shanties" for the migrant laborers who came from the South to work in the sugar beet fields and for the Great Lakes Sugar Company. These structures came complete with a "built-in bed, a small cupboard (shelves, really), even a tiny pot-bellied stove which furnished heat and a small spot for cooking purposes." Many of these structures remained in good condition for decades. Always interested in helping others, Pendleton hired unemployed workers to build the little houses using an assembly-line system.

In the late 1950s, Floyd became ill with a bleeding ulcer, which led to the family's retirement from the company but did not end its involvement. Lois remarked that while they enjoyed traveling and visiting their lake cottage, they knew by 1963 that they were ready to sell the business that they had poured so much into: "We no longer enjoyed a business we weren't really a part of."

M.L. Fassett Lumber Company—Findlay

Lumber and planing mills played an important part in the history of Findlay and Hancock County. One example is Fassett's Lumber Company. It seems that the love of working with wood carried through the life of Hamilton Hiram Fassett. Born in 1846, this farm boy had only a country school education. His father died when Hamilton was only fifteen years old, and two years later, in 1863, he joined the Third Ohio Cavalry, Company 3, and spent much of the rest of the Civil War fighting in the South. After mustering out and returning to his Ohio farm in 1865, he found that he had a natural gift for carpentry and much preferred it to farming.

Not only was Hamilton Fassett considered an expert in cabinetmaking, he also created special-order caskets for undertakers and worked as an undertaker himself for a time when he lived in Baraboo, Wisconsin. He also operated a sawmill in the small town of Curtice, Ohio, for around five years and worked for a brick and tile industry in Martin, Ohio, where he met his future wife, Margaret Allen, a teacher. They were married on June 30, 1887, after moving to Findlay, where Hamilton was self-employed as a carpenter and contractor. He had an office at 525 South Main Street for his hardware and contracting business.

Of Margaret Fassett, Nevin O. Winter, in his book *History of Northwestern Ohio*, wrote: "After her marriage she looked after the duties of her home and the rearing and training of her children, and was an able counselor to her husband in his business affairs." But Margaret was so much more than simply a good wife, mother and counselor. She was an exceptionally strong woman who, throughout her life, stared adversity in the face and carried on.

In 1905, still following his passion for woodworking, Fassett built a factory and planing mill on East Crawford Street. Unfortunately, he did not live long enough to reap the benefits of his new business. His obituary, printed in the *Republican Jeffersonian* on April 24, 1906, states:

> *By trade he was a carpenter, and as a contractor and builder he did much toward making Findlay what it is today. He erected many of the buildings in this city and gave employment, in the aggregate, to a little army of workmen. He leaves a number of fine houses in this city, and in addition had accumulated considerable other property, all earned by the toil of his hands and brain. He was a progressive man in every sense, industrious, and*

never idle for a moment. But disease seized upon his powerful frame, and for the past two or three years he had frequent attacks of illness, and finally succumbed to the fell destroyer.

Margaret took charge of the business and successfully ran it until disaster struck—literally. On August 14, 1909, during a terrible electrical storm in the middle of the night, a fire caused by lightning destroyed the building and the machinery inside. Worse yet, Margaret had no insurance. An article in the August 19, 1909 *Hancock Courier* explained the insurance situation:

> *On the mill and its entire contents of costly lumber and expensive machinery there was at the time of the fire but $1000 of insurance carried. This was due to the fact that on the 20th of July the main bulk of the insurance, which had been carried by the firm expired and had not been renewed. It has always been the policy of Mrs. Fassett, the proprietor, to carry in the neighborhood of $5,000 worth of insurance on the mill and its contents. Again it was her policy to carry the insurance with those of her customers who sold insurance. At the expiration of the policy she put off the renewal of it on account of the fact that she was awaiting an order from one of her patrons in order to know where to place the insurance. The deal was to have been completed this week and the insurance renewed, but before the step was taken the fire came, with a loss of thousands of dollars at a time when the insurance was practically dead.*

Ironically, the flames from the fire barely touched the lumber in the back section of the lumberyard. Valued at $6,000, this batch of wood had several thousand dollars' worth of insurance on it.

The storm itself had awakened much of the population of Findlay. A night man at a livery barn a few doors away from the mill raced to a telephone to call the fire department. Through a series of unfortunate events, the operator notified the central station but either did not or could not reach the north side station or the waterworks at Riverside Park for at least fifteen minutes. In addition, two boilers at the station were out of commission, so a portable boiler was used. A fire engine from the north station arrived and was able to help the situation until a connecting rod broke, putting the engine out of commission, too.

The *Hancock Courier* article continued:

The flames after they had once started spread through the dry timber of the mill and soon the entire building was a solid mass of flames roaring up from between the four walls as from a furnace. Very little headway could be gained by the firemen against this awful onslaught of fire and smoke. With a crash the roof fell sending a shower of sparks up into the night and the storm. Soon the third floor fell and the second, taking with it the machinery and the lumber with a sickening crash. Then began a fight against the solid mass of burning hissing wood piled high inside the bare walls. The fight lasted all through the night and far into the morning it being past noon on Sunday before the water was allowed to stop.

Margaret Fassett had had an uneasy feeling during the night. She thought she smelled smoke from her South Blanchard Street home, even though it was upwind and not near the actual fire. After checking the rooms in her home, she headed back to bed. It was at this time that the telephone rang and she was told that the mill had been struck by lightning and was burning. Her young sons—Guise, Lloyd and Yale—raced to the mill in nightclothes and barefoot and worked throughout the night and into the day battling the blaze. "Yale, the youngest of the children, in going to notify Manager John Shull, fell from his wheel and was painfully injured, which fact he did not make known until after the fire."

In another quirk of fate, the mill at this time carried one of the largest stocks it ever had. Valuable lumber stored on the third floor was valued at $5,000. Cherrywood, sawed oak, cypress and other fine wood and lumber had also been stored there, not to mention unfinished furnishings for two houses and several tons of nails. All were destroyed—a total loss.

The quick thinking and bravery of C.F. Latchaw, Dwight Wertz and Alvin Sheller led to the retrieval of a drawer of important invoices, the main desk, daybooks and carved woodwork that was in the office.

Other losses included between twelve and fifteen new machines on the second floor. The building itself was almost new, having been constructed only three years earlier.

Unfazed, Margaret and her three young sons restored the business and continued to do well. Work to rebuild the factory started in early September 1909. After having to remove all of the debris from the fire, a "carpenter force, six or eight in number, have generously agreed to each donate his services for one week, an act that calls forth much praise, and is keenly appreciated by Mrs. Fassett," the *Republican Jeffersonian* reported. The new building was to be stronger and would have an iron roof. Due to the fact that

Margaret Fassett, proprietor of the M.L. Fassett Lumber Company, expanded her mill when she purchased the Duttweiller Mill on East Crawford Street in 1916. *Courtesy of the Hancock Historical Museum.*

so much of the machinery was destroyed by the fire, most of the equipment at the rebuilt factory would be new.

Not only did Margaret Fassett and her family persevere, but by 1916, she was able to expand the business by buying the Duttweiller Mill, also on East Crawford Street. Besides planing, the M.L. Fassett Lumber Company also built sashes and doors and did interior finish work.

Margaret Fassett, a woman undaunted by her situation who ran a successful business (usually a man's realm) as well as raising her children to be strong and successful, and her family greatly contributed to the community. Her daughter, Charlotte Mae Fassett, lived to be ninety years old and taught school in Findlay for over fifty of those years; she also became president of the M.L. Fassett Lumber Company upon her mother's death in 1925. Another daughter, Helen Fassett Hosman, was an architect in New York and spent much of her career in Detroit. Guise was superintendent and secretary-treasurer of the lumber company. Yale managed the company after Guise's death. And Lloyd seemed to follow in his father's footsteps by becoming a carpenter and also working in construction.

A PART OF THE FURNITURE

A pioneer named Frederick Henderson came from Muskingum County to Hancock County during the summer of 1831 and decided to relocate to Findlay with his wife and child that fall. A cabinetmaker, Henderson plied his trade in downtown Findlay for many years. According to Robert C. Brown, Henderson "was a very successful merchant, and did a large share of the business in his line. Courteous and affable at all times, he won and retained the good will of all with whom he came in contact."

Not only was Henderson a successful tradesperson, he also became quite involved in the community in many different capacities. In December 1831, he and two other early settlers, Wilson Vance and Jonathan Parker, were awarded a contract to build a temporary courthouse for the grand sum of $700, and it was finished in March 1833. Around this time, he was also engaged in helping to create the Benton Ridge road.

Henderson was among the incorporators and served on the board of directors of the Findlay Academical Institute in 1846, and in 1848, he was instrumental in establishing the cemetery association for Maple Grove Cemetery. In addition, he was the first person in the county to receive a business dispatch through the Western Union Telegraph Company in January 1864, two years prior to his death. However, Frederick Henderson was, first and foremost, a "courteous and affable" cabinetmaker who not only built cabinets but also built up the hopes of those who wanted to establish a furniture manufacturing industry in Findlay.

Dietsch Brothers Furniture/Findlay Church Furniture—Findlay

What do church furniture and ice cream have in common? If you answered "nothing," you wouldn't be totally wrong. However, one could argue they share the name Dietsch Brothers. If you have ever lived in or visited Findlay, Ohio, and hear or see those sweet words, "Dietsch Brothers," you are certain to have visions of the many varieties of ice cream and chocolate candy that are handmade and sold at "Dietsch Brothers—Fine Chocolates and Ice Cream." But Findlay was home to another family of Dietsch brothers during the nineteenth century who were better known for creating furniture, not confections.

Born in Ebersdorf, kingdom of Saxony, Edward Dietsch was only eleven years old when he and his family arrived in Findlay. The year was 1849, and the population of Findlay was a mere one thousand people. Edward's father, Charles, a German cabinetmaker, continued that trade and eventually opened a furniture manufacturing enterprise in Findlay. By 1860, Edward, who had also been involved in cabinetmaking, was ready to join his father in the family business, which became Charles Dietsch & Son. Ten years later, Edward's younger brother Anthony joined the partnership, and the company's name was changed to A. Dietsch & Company.

At first, the business was housed in a frame building at the corner of Liberty and West Main Cross Streets. But in 1876, a larger, three-story brick building was erected and became known as the Dietsch Block.

Following Charles's death in early 1883, a notice appeared in the *Findlay Daily Jeffersonian*, strongly encouraging

> *all persons knowing themselves indebted to the firm of A. Dietsch & Co. will settle their accounts promptly, as the death of Charles Dietsch, of said firm, makes a settlement necessary. All accounts not settled by April 1st, will be in the collector's hands. The old firm return their thanks for the very liberal patronage extended to them. The new firm will be DIETSCH BROTHERS, who, by strict attention to business, hope to merit the favors of the community in the future as the old firm has in the past.*

Even before the gas and oil booms of the late 1880s and 1890s, Dietsch Brothers was doing "booming" business, with ten employees and averaging around $10,000 a year in sales. At one point, they supplied the new Findlay College with laboratory tables in the chemistry department.

Dietsch Brothers Furniture Company erected this three-story brick building on West Main Cross Street in Findlay in 1876. *Courtesy of the Hancock Historical Museum.*

However, by the late 1880s, Edward had sold his interest in Dietsch Brothers Furniture to Anthony in order to start another furniture venture: Findlay Church Furniture Factory. In October 1887, the *Daily Courier* predicted "this new manufacturing enterprise would become an important industry to Findlay" and praised Edward Dietsch as manager, noting, "as he is one of the best cabinetmakers and workers in wood in the State, the management will be in good hands."

For several years, Dietsch Brothers had been manufacturing church pews and furniture and bank fixtures in addition to household furnishings, but their furniture factory simply wasn't large enough to do the kind of work that needed to be done or fill the many orders they were receiving.

In January 1888, the *Findlay Weekly Republican* reported: "The Findlay Church Furniture Factory has begun operations at the new factory on West Lima Street. Its sixty-horsepower engine was started just ninety days after the location was decided on. It will one day be one of Findlay's important industries."

The three-story factory, located on about two acres at the corner of West Lima and Ninth Streets, was forty feet by seventy feet, with a cooling fountain in front of it. Edward Dietsch's first-floor office faced West Lima Street, and anyone wanting to see what the factory offered could browse the samples of church pews, mantelpieces and pulpits. In addition, the factory

F. W. FIRMIN, Prest.   F. B. ZAY, Sec'y.   J. W. ZELLER, Vice-Prest.
C. E. NILES, Treas.   E. DIETSCH, Gen'l Mgr.

THE FINDLAY
Church Furniture Manufacturing Co.

By utilizing the advantages offered manufacturers
in the use of

FREE GAS FOR FUEL,

Specially Invented Machinery,

Devised for the Saving of Labor in this business and Economy
in Management, we are enabled to compete successfully
in our estimates for

FURNISHING CHURCHES, HALLS, ETC.

**See our Work and Get Prices Before
Contracting.**

OFFICE AND FACTORY:
Cor. Lima and Ninth Streets and L. E. & W. R. R.

We also design and make WOOD MANTELS of every de-
scription, style and finish equal to any in the market.

In 1887, Edward Dietsch left Dietsch Brothers to establish the Findlay Church Furniture factory on West Lima and Ninth Streets, while his brother Anthony retained Dietsch Brothers Furniture. *Courtesy of the Hancock Historical Museum.*

took orders for school furniture. As the *Findlay Weekly Republican* mentioned in July 1888, "The designing is done by Mr. Dietsch and is not only original but genuinely artistic."

Not only did the new factory go through many expansions over the next few years, Dietsch's company also built six "double dwelling houses" to accommodate some of the workers. The workforce started out with twelve men but was expected to be increased as the building itself expanded.

One of the many assignments fulfilled by the Findlay Church Furniture Factory included making pews and a pulpit for the new Howard M.E. Church on Cherry Street—a church that is still active today. The *Hancock Courier* reported on the church's dedication in July 1888: "The Findlay Church Furniture Co. has furnished the building with comfortable pews and an elegant pulpit. The pews are of ash with black walnut trimmings, and the pulpit of black walnut." Classrooms were also outfitted with chairs.

Business was good, and it was not limited to Findlay. In 1889, the Findlay Church Furniture Manufacturing Company held the contract to furnish seats for the new United Brethren church in Fostoria. It also bested more than five competitors for a contract with the Third Presbyterian Church of Toledo, "one of the finest church edifices in Ohio," according to the *Hancock Courier*. In addition, it provided the seating for the Methodist church in Delta, in Fulton County.

In August 1889, Mother Nature played havoc with the Findlay Church Furniture Factory, blowing off the iron roof and drenching hundreds of dollars' worth of finished furniture. By the following year, however, the factory was again expanding and expecting to double its capacity and triple its business. In fact, the calendar for 1891 had already been completely filled "at good prices."

In 1894, the Findlay Church Furniture Factory received a $4,000 contract to seat the new St. Vincent's Catholic Church in Brooklyn, New York, in "the handsomest design the company has ever produced, of polished oak."

Anthony was also doing well with Dietsch Brothers, advertising in the spring of 1891:

> *The citizens of Findlay and surrounding country should bear in mind that the Dietsch Furniture store is on West Main-Cross street, the third block west of the Court House, where you will find an elegant new stock which I am receiving in place of the goods that will be removed. Respectfully, A. Dietsch, 330 and 332 West Main-Cross street.*

The Dietsch Brothers Furniture building in the 1970s. *Courtesy of the Hancock Historical Museum.*

The June 22, 1906 *Republican Jeffersonian* celebrated the Dietsch family, which had come to Findlay fifty-seven years earlier. Both Edward and Anthony were deceased by this time. However, a grandson of Anthony "conducts a confectionary," the article stated. And grandsons of Edward were instrumental in starting the Dietsch Brothers—Fine Chocolates and Ice Cream shop, which is located just a few doors away from the original furniture store at 400 West Main Cross Street. So, if someone asks you what furniture and ice cream have in common, perhaps you could respond, "cherry and walnut."

FINDLAY TABLE MANUFACTURING COMPANY— FINDLAY

Another furniture factory that made its debut in Findlay during the boom of the 1880s was the Findlay Table factory. It was located at the corner of Frey and Factory Streets between Lima Street and Lima Avenue—just a few blocks from the Findlay Church Furniture Factory, in fact.

The plant began with a large workforce in January 1887, and by April, twenty-five more men had been hired, increasing capacity by half. By October 1888, the factory was producing and shipping one hundred tables a day. Eventually, this factory, run by Louis Heusner, J.W. Andregg and William J. Heusner, employed eighty men.

The factory prospered for many years, even adding a well that allowed ice-cold water to supply the entire building. The well had been dug in 1899 to a depth of fifty-five feet. A donkey engine, a kind of small steam engine usually used for lifting things, was employed to force the water through the building. Since water was also used in the factory's boilers, management found they were able to save money in the long run.

Long after the gas and oil boom had fizzled and many factories had abandoned Findlay, the Findlay Table Manufacturing Company, also referred to as the Findlay Table Factory, was still producing and selling like never before. In 1906, the *Republican Jeffersonian* reported: "The Findlay Table Factory is probably one of the busiest centers in the city at present. For many weeks the orders have been coming in so rapidly that the management has been unable to fill them on time. This factory employs a little army of men and will shortly give employment to more." At one point, employees worked all night in order to rush an order of two train carloads of tables to San Francisco.

Cold weather, deaths and unfortunate occurrences also caused some problems for the factory. Extreme cold one year caused a temporary shutdown. Another time, the death of a manager's father closed the factory for several days. A non-delivery of coal from Fostoria caused another multiple-day shutdown. One of the worst things that happened involved a night watchman who nearly suffocated. As the *Republican Jeffersonian* reported on September 15, 1906:

> *The night watchman at the Findlay table factory had an experience one night this week that he will never forget, and which caused him to throw up his job the next day.*
>
> *The watchman's name is Neier, and he was going his rounds during the night, when he stepped into what is known as the sawdust box. The box is closed by a trap door, which closes with a snap.*
>
> *After Neier had entered the box the door fell into place, to his horror, and he was a prisoner. The full force of his position suddenly flashed upon him, and he at once set to work to get out. This he found was easier thought of than done. The closing of the door caused the box to become*

virtually airtight, and the heat caused by the sawdust was something fierce, almost intolerable.

Neier worked like a trojan to open the door, and the perspiration poured off him in streams. He became desperate, and finally after an almost maniacal effort, succeeded in bursting his way out of the room and into the fresh air. He was almost exhausted, and as "weak as a cat," but thankful that he was alive. As stated, he resigned his position next day.

Two years later, the factory continued to improve and exceed expectations. In 1908, about forty-five men worked there, and officials expected to increase the workforce soon. The factory had enough orders in June of that year to be able to run several months "without taking a single new order. Desperate efforts are being made to fill the New York orders, the plant working all day and at night up to ten o'clock," according to the June 4, 1908 *Republican Jeffersonian.* The company's quality dining room tables were shipped to customers all over the United States. Four train cars per week carried the products via the Lake Erie & Western Railroad; other roads were used for lesser amounts of merchandise.

The Findlay Table Manufacturing Company went into receivership in 1914. The building itself, however, was soon put to use as a churn factory and eventually became part of the Grant Motor Company factory. In 1919, the Giant Tire and Rubber company bought the Faultless Anchor and Manufacturing company's property, "formerly known as the Findlay Table factory on Western avenue," as reported in the *Weekly Jeffersonian.*

Opp House Saloon/Apostolic School and Temple—Findlay

In the late 1880s, Findlay was home to many saloons, taverns, hotels and eateries—this is still true today, but back then, it was a new phenomenon brought about by the influx of gas and oil workers and their families. One establishment, a large brick building in the 400 block of East Sandusky Street, was known as the Opp Block. Willoughby Frederick Opp, a colorful character who seemed to be on the wrong side of the law more often than not, owned the block and operated a saloon, billiard hall and hotel there.

Opp's tenure as saloonkeeper can be summarized in terms like indictment, bankruptcy, arrest, fights, scandals and foul language. His most frequent offenses had to do with selling alcohol on Sunday, a violation of a local liquor ordinance. As one newspaper put it, he was arrested "for selling intoxicating liquor to a person in the habit of becoming intoxicated"—this happened over and over again. Meeting with the mayor or judge and pleading "not guilty" most of the time, Opp often avoided jail and sometimes got just plain lucky. In 1892, for example, he was arrested and arraigned, with a trial set for September. The next month, he was tried once before the mayor with a result he had faced before—a hung jury. "The jury was out five hours, first standing 9 to 3 in favor of conviction then 8 to 4 and afterwards 10 to 2," reported the Findlay *Morning Republican*. "They hung until they were satisfied that there was no chance of an agreement and so reported and were discharged." Incidentally, in 1890, the Dow Liquor Tax led to the closing or selling of many area saloons. Willoughby Opp sold out to John H. Opp at that time but maintained his position as proprietor (and abuser) of the Sunday laws.

Fast-forward to 1907 to see what can happen to a "sinful" establishment full of billiard tables, liquor shelves, bar counters and more than twenty rooms over the saloon when frugality, ingenuity and faith play a role. Enter

The Opp Block, located in the 400 block of East Sandusky Street, was once home to a saloon and a church. *Courtesy of the author.*

Reverend Thomas K. Leonard, who purchased the Opp Block from John Opp in January of that year.

Reverend Leonard was born in 1861 in West Independence, a small community in Hancock County about twelve miles east of Findlay. Growing up, he faced many personal tragedies, losing family members to tuberculosis and diphtheria, but he had an abiding faith in God, to which he credited his mother's devotion. This faith led him to Findlay College in 1892 to study "theology and elocution."

The years between 1894 and 1906 found him leading camp meetings and revivals, as well as pastoring three churches in the county. He owned a large farm near McComb but found that something more spiritual was pulling him to get rid of his possessions and search for a place to spread the gospel.

Leonard had led revivals in Findlay in the past and felt that a mission there would be an important step in furthering his Pentecostal message of the Christian Union. He felt he had the financial support necessary to succeed in this endeavor. In January 1907, he purchased the old Opp Hotel, the two-story building that housed a saloon on the first floor and, reputedly, a brothel on the second, for $5,000, although its value was closer to $20,000. His dreams for the building included a complete renovation to create a Bible school, a church, a printing shop and office space. Unfortunately for him, however, his colleagues and would-be financial backers did not agree with his grandiose ideas and dropped him like a bad habit—except one man, Owen Eugene McCleary, who was also involved with the Christian Union. The two of them were left with their ideas, the building and the debt.

Their faith, frugality and ingenuity led to the establishment of the Apostolic School, the Apostolic Temple, and the *Apostolic Herald*, all interdenominational as well as interracial.

In March 1907, the *Republican Jeffersonian* reported in lavish terms about the block's transformation from saloon to house of God, crediting Leonard and McCleary with their eternal determination to be successful. The article describes the creative and complex "makeover," pointing out that a "large force of carpenters, painters and paper hangers are busily engaged in repairing the rooms, getting them ready for the first meeting that is to be held there, March 14, and beautifying the exterior with a new coat of paint, thus obliterating the old tobacco and liquor signs on the east wall."

The piece goes on to explain that the twenty-three rooms on the second floor would be reconfigured and used as a dormitory and a library. The first floor, then, would be used as the office and storage area for sacred books, with the "booze" shelves being utilized to hold sacred literature and the bar counter to be employed as the bookstore counter. Additional renovations included repurposing things like slot machines, pool cues, billiard tables and card tables:

> There were two large penny card slot machines left in the building and these will be put to very good use. One of them will be transformed into a pulpit for the 'temple' and the other will be re-arranged so that when the lever is pressed for the wheel to revolve, cards with scriptural quotations and religious cartoons will appear in place of the playing cards.

In addition, free-will offerings would be deposited in a small nickel-slot machine, and the beautifully polished wild cherry bar counter rail would enclose the altar in front of the pulpit. At one time, two glass cases in the saloon held whiskey and rye signs—not anymore. They were soon set out in front of the building to announce church meetings. The *Jeffersonian* article continued:

> Another distinguishing peculiarity about the new arrangement will be the card tables turned into communion tables, and the tops of the billiard tables used as composing stones for the publishing department. The billiard cues will be used as handles for the collection baskets, which in turn will be made from the pockets of the pool tables.

The saloon had had a small elevator-type shaft connecting the first and second floors, most likely used for carrying food and drink. The new church would use this convenience to connect the editorial rooms with the composing room. A baptismal dressing room and laboratory were to be made from a small closet not far from the bar. And the large barroom mirrors from the wine case were to be moved into the dining area.

T.K. Leonard had published the *Christian Unity Herald* in McComb and decided to build a printing room on the first floor of the new enterprise to print the *Apostolic Herald*, which eventually became the *Christian Gospel Herald*. A large room, sixty by twenty feet, was partitioned to include room for printing presses and type that were used in McComb and had been stored in a building on Crawford Street. In addition, part of the partitioned room would contain a kitchen and a dining room.

The primary focuses in the "Temple," a large area on the east side of the first floor, would be a raised pulpit, piano and an organ. The thirty-by-eighty-foot space would hold up to 250 people. In the floor of the pulpit's

Pentecostal Convention

OF THE

ASSEMBLY OF GOD

WILL CONVENE AT

THE APOSTOLIC SCHOOL,

Findlay, Ohio, Dec. 24th. to Jan. 1st. 1909.

WE RECOGNIZE that the general ASSEMBLY (Church or Kingdom) OF GOD, built and established in the world by Jesus Christ consists of all Christians (irrespective of denominational distinction) who are born of God and by the one Spirit baptized into the one body or household of God whose names are written in Heaven. See, Mat. 16: 18; John 3:3; 1 John 3:8-10 Eph. 2: 19; 1 Cor.12: 13. Heb.12:23; Mat. 3; 2; 6- 33; Col. 1: 12, 18, Hence, all are welcome and invited.

A local Assembly of God consists of a congregation of the general Assembly or Kingdom of God who are drawn together, set in order and united by the Holy Spirit in regular worship in any city or locality. See Rev. third chapter.

THESE MEETINGS will stand for Bible Salvation and Pentecostal Power in its fulness. To this end the Holy Ghost, the Gifts of the Spirit, and all that glorifies Jesus will be given place. COME HUNGRY ONE and Tarry until you be endued with power from on high.

ACCOMMODATIONS.

THE AUDITORIUM has a seating capacity of nearly 300.

THE UPPER ROOM consists of two large rooms affording space inside and for workers and workers only.

LOCATION—At 404-406 East Sandusky street, by the T. & O. C. Depot, one square from Big Four depot, four squares from Court House.

RAILROADS—Findlay has the following: Toledo, Ohio Central, Big Four, Lake Erie & Western, C. H. & D, Findlay, Ft. Wayne & Western, Nickel Plate, get off at Mortimer, take Electric car to Sandusky street; Baltimore & Ohio, get off at Galatea, take Ohio Central to Findlay; Pennsylvania Lines via Ohio Central, Dunkirk, O.

ELECTRIC LINES—Toledo, Bowling Green & Southern, Western Ohio, Toledo, Fostoria & Findlay.

MEALS and Lunches will be served at reasonable prices.

LODGING—We can furnish cots for 75 or 50 persons. Each person must bring necessary bed clothing. We shall register names for accommodations in the order they reach us, so write us early. Beds and cots at ten cents per night.

For further information write THE APOSTOLIC HERALD, Findlay, Ohio, U. S. A.

BELL PHONE, 312.K.

COME, TARRY, RECEIVE THE PROMISE.

The Opp House became the Apostolic School and the Apostolic Temple in 1907. *Courtesy of the Hancock Historical Museum.*

raised platform was "a large door which opens to a fine cement reservoir for baptismal purposes. The reservoir will be furnished with city water, heated by the church's furnace, which in turn is supplied with gas from a well under the building."

The Apostolic School became the Apostolic Gospel School in 1909 and the Gospel School from 1911 until 1930. Reverend Leonard continued to minister until he retired as pastor in 1941 at age eighty. Although he had planned to continue teaching and evangelizing, dementia robbed him of those activities. He died in 1946, and a year later, his wife of fifty-six years passed away.

Diller's Furniture/Bennett Brothers Furniture Company—McComb

Another longtime fixture in Hancock County began in the early part of the twentieth century when Frank and Menno Diller, two brothers from Bluffton, Ohio, decided to organize a furniture business. By 1910, they had set up their business in a building on Main Street in downtown McComb. Early on, of course, delivering furniture to area residents meant using a horse and wagon, which was difficult work. Not to be deterred, however, the brothers continued to grow their business and gain customers from around the countryside.

Eventually, Frank bought out Menno's share of the business and continued as sole proprietor. He married Pearl Perry in 1909, and together, they built a long-lasting family partnership. They had two sons, Wade and Eugene, and a daughter, Winifred. When he was old enough, Eugene became an integral part of the business.

Much of the furniture the Dillers sold came from annual furniture shows in places like Chicago. During the early 1900s, that city was slowly climbing out of the depression that had hit in the previous decade and wreaked havoc with small furniture concerns owned by immigrants. Larger, more upscale factories began to appear. Between 1900 and 1910, the number of furniture plants in Chicago had expanded from one hundred to two hundred, with the workforce extending from an average of seventy workers per plant to over ten thousand per plant. Chicago had the advantage of being a substantial city center in proximity to railroad transportation and, later, roadways, as well as being influential in the finance and marketing businesses. As described in the *Encyclopedia of Chicago History*: "In the early 1920s, Illinois ranked second only to New York in value of furniture produced, and Chicago dominated the state's furniture industry."

The furniture manufacturers in Chicago rallied around and began a marketing campaign that reached the entire country. They started organizing annual trade shows, and these were the shows that the Dillers attended year after year to find the latest styles and trends in furniture.

In January 1928, the *McComb Herald* announced:

> *Mr. and Mrs. Frank Diller left today for Chicago to attend the Chicago-Grand Rapids furniture market and the Diller furniture store will be open only after school until their return. From this gathering the advancing trend of furniture is determined, for style is the greatest single factor in selling*

today. Furniture, like automobiles, is style goods, and is both comfort and friendship. This idea is emphasized as being uppermost in 1928.

President Calvin Coolidge even had a hand in the festivities, lighting up two miles of furniture exhibits by pressing a gold button in the White House.

Although the Great Depression touched the Dillers, as it did almost everyone in the country, they made it through, and business continued to thrive. In fact, in 1935, they were moving their second Diller's Furniture store, this one in Findlay, from the Phoenix Block at the corner of South Main and Main Cross Streets, where it had been for two years, to 320 North Main Street.

Along came World War II, and the two Diller sons, Eugene and Wade, headed off to serve their country. Their father, Frank, felt the heavy heart of one waiting for loved ones to come home safely. In April 1943, he placed a large advertisement in the *Findlay Republican Courier* to let his customers know that Diller's Furniture Company "will fold up for 'the duration,' due to Eugene's being in Midshipman's School at Notre Dame and Wade, a Toledo lawyer, waiting for word of where he would be going." Frank did not want to be the lone manager of the store in the event that his sons did not return. He promised, though, that if they did return, the family would restock their six buildings with furniture and continue the business.

Diller's Furniture Company successfully managed the "duration" and was back in business by 1946, after Eugene and his wife and child returned to McComb. That same year, Eugene was awarded a naval commendation citation for his "unusual competence, constant diligence, and unfailing devotion to duty." He had been communication watch officer on the staff of an amphibious group in the Pacific theater from 1943 to 1945.

In March 1946, the *Hancock Herald* reported: "The Diller Furniture Store resumed business this week, after having been closed for the past three years because of war conditions. Eugene Diller has put in a new stock of merchandise and will enlarge the selection and items offered as they become available."

The next several years saw many changes in the personal lives of the Dillers. Eugene's mother, Pearl, passed away after a lengthy illness in December 1947. About six months later, Frank Diller suffered a heart attack while on his way home from a Rotary International convention in Rio de Janeiro. He was at a hotel in San Juan, Puerto Rico, writing a letter to Eugene, when he succumbed to the attack.

Although Frank had retired from active work in the furniture business, he had still been, at age seventy-two, quite committed to Rotary, having been a member for many years and attended Rotary International conventions in the United States and Europe.

In 1953, Eugene Diller sold Diller's Furniture in McComb, eventually starting another furniture store in Lima, which has expanded several times and is now operated by fourth-generation Dillers.

Eugene's brother-in-law Edward "Ned" Bennett and Ned's brother Dan purchased Diller's Furniture in late 1953. An ad in the *Findlay Republican Courier* stated, "In the future the Diller Furniture Co. will be known as 'Bennett Brothers Furniture Co.' owned and operated by Edw. (Ned) Bennett, part owner for the past 7 years and Dan Bennett, associated with Diller's for the past 7 years. We have taken complete inventory of our huge stock and have decided the following items must go regardless of price." A long list of items drastically reduced in price by up to 65 percent followed the announcement.

A short two years later, Bennett Brothers Furniture Company was expanding its display and sales services. More room was needed for the

Diller's Furniture and Bennett Brothers Furniture occupied much of downtown McComb over the years. *Courtesy of the Hancock Historical Museum.*

expanding inventory, so the Bennetts bought a building a few doors down from the original building—this was just the beginning.

Not only did Bennett Brothers sell furniture, it also had departments featuring carpeting, appliances, mattresses, upholstery and window treatments. Charles "Chuck" Wasson began at Bennett Brothers as manager of the carpet department around 1959.

Chuck's son Joe remembers many stories about the store during the 1960s and 1970s, when he was a youngster. "Back then," he states, "there was nowhere to shop for furniture like there is today." Before the big-box stores invaded the area, furniture was sold from furniture stores. And the furniture at Bennett Brothers came from all over, not just from Chicago. For example, store management traveled to North Carolina twice a year to add to the inventory.

At that time, the store's delivery area included all of northwest Ohio within a one-hundred-mile radius; this included Toledo, Findlay, Lima and even southern Michigan. In order serve this area, many delivery trucks had to make multiple deliveries per day. "I remember stories," says Joe, "of how full the delivery trucks would be and these guys not getting home until eleven or twelve at night and making two or three trips a day, just to get all this furniture out." Bennett Brothers Furniture Company's operating hours at that time did not include Sundays. It was open from 9:00 a.m. to 9:00 p.m., Monday through Saturday, with a "suppertime" closing from 5:00 to 7:00 p.m.

In the late 1970s, many of the smaller "mom-and-pop" shops in McComb began closing, probably with the onset of the big-box stores coming to the area. However, Bennett Brothers continued to grow in the village itself by purchasing these closing businesses.

During these years, the Bennett "family" became very close. Many of the employees, related not only by blood but also by common experience, had been with the company for decades. It came as a great shock, then, when word came of Ned Bennett's unexpected passing due to a probable heart attack at his Florida home in December 1978.

By the early 1980s, Bennett Brothers owned sixteen buildings—individual storefronts—on Main Street in McComb. As buildings were purchased, many walls were demolished in order to create larger showrooms. In time, six buildings became home to a new Broyhill Gallery, and much remodeling and updating was done.

In 1984, Dan was also taken from the family, by cancer. His wife, Daisy, took ownership of the store, continuing the store's success and expansions until her death in 1996. Since none of the Bennetts had children, Daisy was

In the 1980s, the Bennett brothers owned sixteen buildings on Main Street in McComb for their furniture business. *Courtesy of the Hancock Historical Museum.*

the final person in the line of ownership. The Bennett Brothers Furniture Company trust sought to either sell or liquidate the business.

Joe Wasson had become a salesperson for the company when he joined the business in 1992. His father, Chuck, had become manager of operations in 1995. After Daisy's death, Joe and Chuck did some heavy soul-searching. Should they buy the business or not? After all, Chuck was in his midsixties and did not really want the headaches that came with purchasing the company, but he felt that Joe was young enough to continue the business. In the end, in 1996, together, they purchased Bennett Brothers Furniture Company, keeping the well-known name of the store.

Business operated as usual for many years. However, the 2008 recession hit them hard, and they never fully recovered, although they "weathered it and got through it," Joe explained.

Unfortunately, by 2012, the business was still struggling, and Chuck Wasson had died. Joe and his wife "had a conversation," deciding that it was time to sell or liquidate the business rather than face the financial burden that continuing the stores would inflict. Bennett Brothers Furniture Company (and the ghosts of Diller's Furniture) closed in July 2013 after over a century of serving the furniture needs of McComb, northwest Ohio and lower Michigan.

PART 4: GETTING FROM HERE TO THERE—TRANSPORTATION

1

THEY MISSED THE TRAIN

A veritable alphabet soup of railroads began crisscrossing Hancock County during the second half of the nineteenth century: AC&Y, CCC&SL (the Big 4), CD&SL, CH&D, FF&W, LE&W, MR&LE, TC&C, NPK, NO, NYC&SL, SD&C, T&OC. These connected cities like Akron, Canton, Chicago, Cincinnati, Cleveland, Columbus, Dayton, Findlay, Fort Wayne, Hamilton, New York, Toledo, Youngstown and places like Northern Ohio, Mad River and Lake Erie. The Nickel Plate was the nickname of one line.

When the railroads arrived in Hancock County, many a community was born. Findlay and Fostoria, the two "cities" in Hancock County today (although Fostoria is actually in three different counties) fared well—they flourished and grew. Other towns and villages that welcomed train traffic may not have grown into big cities, but they were grateful for the positive results spurred by the arrival of the railroad. Mt. Cory, Rawson, McComb, Arcadia, Jenera, Arlington, Mt. Blanchard and Vanlue all benefited by being on the railroad line and are still around today. But other settlements, although they may have started with a station or a depot, were unable to thrive and eventually ceased to exist. Yes, they missed the train.

The Cincinnati, Hamilton & Dayton (CH&D) Railway came into centrally located Findlay from the northwest corner of the county, passing through Hancock, Deweyville, McComb, Conine, Murphy's Siding and Chase. McComb is the only town today of any size, at around 1,600 residents. The Findlay Branch of the Big Four (Cleveland, Cincinnati, Chicago & St. Louis

Mt. Blanchard was one of many towns in Hancock County located along various railroad lines. Most of the old depots have been razed; some have been repurposed, like the Rawson depot, which is now part of Rawson Park. *Courtesy of the Hancock Historical Museum.*

or CCC&SL) continued southeast from Findlay to Vanlue, with a station about halfway between them at the community of Huber that was in use for only a short time.

The Lake Erie & Western (LE&W) crossed the county from southwest to northeast, going through Dennis, Mt. Cory, Rawson, Willow Creek, Findlay, Marion and Arcadia on the way to Fostoria. Willow Creek was considered a "flag stop," meaning the train would only stop if someone signaled it.

Crossing the northern part of the county from west to east, the Nickel Plate Railway (NKP) went through Shawtown, McComb, Stuartsville and Arcadia to Fostoria.

The southern area of the county had the Northern Ohio (NO) Railroad, which traveled from west to east through Langan, El Rose, Cordelia (a.k.a. Cordelta), Jenera, Arlington and Mt. Blanchard before heading northeast toward Vanlue through Pratts.

Cutting the county in half from north to south was the Toledo and Ohio Central (T&OC). Towns like Van Buren, Mortimer (a.k.a. North Findlay), Findlay, Beagle and Arlington could be found along this route.

Finally, crossing the center of the county was one of the straightest railroads in the country at that time: the Findlay, Ft. Wayne & Western (FF&W). It passed Moffitt and Benton before reaching Findlay.

MOFFITT STATION

Moffitt Station was a town that really wasn't. The Moffitt family owned a large parcel of farmland in western Blanchard Township. In 1889, Demetrius Moffitt, Curtis Moffit, N.B. McClish and M.E. Hopkins signed and had notarized a plat map and notes describing the acreage, lots, avenues, streets, and alleys they proposed would become "Moffitt Station." Nearly one hundred lots were laid out (on paper, anyway) along Main, Harrison and West Streets and Hopkins, Park and McClish Avenues. Railroad Street bisected the proposed town, with a depot and an elevator to be located on either side of the railroad tracks. Moffitt was a stop on the American Midland Railroad, which later became the FF&W, but a depot was never built, nor were any lots developed.

In January 1895, however, the *Daily Courier* noted that foundations had been built for a new elevator and warehouse following the construction of a corncrib a few weeks earlier. "The crib will hold 10,000 bushels," according to the article. The elevator lasted about twenty-four years before being purchased and moved to Findlay in 1919.

There really was a community at Moffitt Station, it just wasn't a big town. People in Moffitt Station read the *Courier*, which covered not only their community but other outlying small areas, such as Shawtown and Deweyville. One 1913 article mentioned that because of the *Courier*'s circulation throughout the county, the sheriff was able to find two people who had read that he had a summons for them but did not know where they lived. The sheriff was "fairly over-joyed to realize that his search was over." And the *Courier* maintained that this was "evidence of the great degree of intelligence of the people of Moffitt Station and vicinity."

Moffitt Station was a "hive of industry" in 1916, when roads in the area were being improved. Trucks delivered tons of stone each day as men worked night and day to build a better roadway. As the *Weekly Jeffersonian* stated, "Moffitt Station is no more a sleepy little hamlet."

A "native" of Moffitt Station—"I lived the first twenty-two years of my life there"—Jack Ridge tells of his grandparents moving to Moffitt Station in the early 1920s, when Jack's father was twelve, and buying a grocery there. They also farmed a 360-acre spread.

Moffitt Station and Benton Station (a bit north of Benton Ridge, about three miles from Moffitt Station) were both on the FF&W Railroad. Now, the railroad is "just a hump in the road," as Ridge described it. Vestiges of the railroad—gravel and the base—remained for some time, even though it was abandoned in 1919.

"I remember my dad and grandfather talking about the record set in Moffitt Station for the number of cattle shipped in one day," Ridge says. At that time, in the early part of the twentieth century, farmers' fields were fenced, so when it was time to drive (meaning walk) the cattle from their farms to the train station, farmers simply traveled with them on the roads. Women stood by the roads, waving their aprons so the cows would stay out of their yards and gardens. Cattle "were lined up way down the road, waiting to get them to the scale and loaded on the railroad. It must have been quite a sight."

The *Weekly Jeffersonian* documented this event on February 21, 1901. "Jap Dukes, of Blanchard township, one of the most prominent stock buyers in Northern Ohio, on Wednesday shipped forty cars of cattle from Moffitt Station. They were shipped direct to New York where they will be put on board ships and transported to England. Mr. Dukes raised several cars of the cattle on his own farm." Forty railroad cars of cattle!

Jack Ridge remembers only four houses in Moffitt Station but said people from miles around would come to the grocery store. Not only could they buy groceries or trade eggs and cream for food, but the store was the "happening" place, especially on Fridays and Saturdays. "It was a social gathering area for people," he said. Watching Friday night fights on television was a "big event." His grandfather had one of the "first TVs in captivity" and would tune in to *Big Time Wrestling*, and the evening was set. Sometimes, when the men arrived with the intent of purchasing groceries and then immediately going home, they would become sidetracked watching the fights or playing pool, getting home much later than their wives felt was appropriate. One woman, in fact, "prayed that the store would burn down" so her husband wouldn't have a place to play pool.

"Community spirit is something you had in Moffitt Station," Ridge stated. He grew up with the story about his grandfather during the Great Depression in the early 1930s. Everyone was experiencing hard times. But his grandfather, who was facing possible bankruptcy, "had such a big heart, if people came in to the store and needed something and couldn't pay, he'd give them credit." However, he gave them so much credit that he was unable to meet his own bills. Two area farmers who knew of his plight underwrote his debt. "They knew who he was and what he was doing. He wasn't getting rich by not paying his bills; he was giving food to people who needed it." Ridge noted the "connectedness of little towns" and appreciated growing up in that environment.

2

NOW YOU'RE ON THE TROLLEY

Because of the intense illumination produced by the natural gas and oil wells, day and night, Findlay earned several nicknames, including "City of Light" and "Brilliant City." The gas and oil boom of the late 1880s brought thousands of people to Findlay, creating the need for accessible transportation routes. Many manufacturers lured to "Brilliant City" by the free fuel and land offers located their factories on the outskirts of the city, where land was plentiful. At that time, downtown Findlay was already erecting new buildings or remodeling old ones along Main Street, and talk of a streetcar railway system was taking shape. In fact, the Findlay Street Railway Company had been formed by 1887.

However, according to the *Hancock Courier*, convincing the city council that "Findlay wants a street car system and wants it bad" proved to be difficult, as "none of the members of the council had ever had any experience in the matter of Street Railways." The big question facing them involved the power source. Should the cars be horse- or mule-drawn, or should electricity provide the "pull"? A New Yorker named S.T. Dunham was at first granted the franchise to build a railway through downtown Findlay that probably would have been electrically powered, like the one he had built in Mansfield, Ohio. Councilmen were invited to travel to Mansfield to get a better idea of how the system worked, but apparently, no one had the time to spare, and Dunham's franchise was eventually revoked.

Instead, a new ordinance was passed, and George P. Kerper, from Cincinnati, was granted the franchise. Other franchises would also be granted to other areas of the city. For example, Freeman Thorpe, A.P. Byal, B.H. Rickard and W.A. Byal were granted a franchise to build a street railway on Lima Street from Main Street to Lima Road. The *Findlay Weekly Republican* expressed its views of the early stages of the streetcar system with regret that the city council had not responded the previous spring when approached about the streetcar concept: "Had this been done, by this time we would have had a cable road in operation and the city would have had at least 4000 more people as inhabitants than it has today."

Tracks were laid throughout Findlay—north and south, east and west—and by late 1888, the city had over sixteen miles of street railway track. This included three miles on the West Park line, eight on Main Street, two and a half on the Wyoming Place line that went to the Dalzell factory in northwestern Findlay and three miles on the Blanchard Avenue line. Other lines soon to be up and running included the Cemetery line, an extension on South Main Street and a line on Tiffin Avenue.

It was not long before the horse- and mule-drawn cars were replaced by electric cars. In June 1891, the *Daily Courier* announced: "Findlay, the Brilliant City, whose progress and fame has exceeded that of any contemporaneous city in the country, has taken another big stride, and added to the long list of her substantial, permanent improvements, in the opening of the finest electric railway system in the United States." President George Kerper and Superintendent Charles Smith, of the Findlay Street Railway Company, invited "officials of the city and county and many prominent citizens" to inspect the brick powerhouse west of Main Street. "Two beautiful, powerful engines were spinning as noiselessly as the movements of the heavenly bodies in space, driving a pair of enormous dynamos which generated the electricity for use on the ten miles of wire."

The novelty of electricity amazed the visitors—especially the reporter, it seems. "After a complete examination of this really interesting but at the same time mysterious apparatus, where the lightnings of the heavens are brought down, coiled up, inducted and let loose at the will of the electrician in charge, to work miracles in setting in rapid motion the wheels of heavy chariots," the group was treated to lemonade and champagne punch.

Following a few short speeches about this wonderful new mode of transportation, visitors had the opportunity to take a ride through town, with the Elks' Northwestern Band furnishing music. "Two of the elegant new motor cars had been run out from the barn, and to one of these was attached one of the new summer cars." First, they traveled south to Chamberlin Hill.

There, the cars were put on the return track and headed for Bigelow Hill, five miles to the north, reaching it in twenty-three minutes.

According to the reporter, the rails were smooth, and the cars were quiet: "The cars themselves are of the latest patterns, elegantly finished, and as complete in every respect as can be found upon any line in the United States. Three incandescent lights beautifully illuminate the interior at night."

A new electric line between Findlay and Fostoria was proposed in 1899, to be constructed along Fostoria Road. In Findlay, this interurban line would join the existing streetcar line. Eventually, the tracks would be extended entirely across the northern part of Ohio from Cleveland to Indiana.

The following year, the Toledo, Fostoria & Findlay (TF&F) Electric Railway people built a powerhouse in Fostoria, and workmen were readying ties to be laid. Also, plans were being made to establish another trolley line to connect Findlay and Lima, with a route through Bluffton, Mt. Cory and Rawson.

The TF&F line was up and running in 1901. These state-of-the-art cars came complete with telephones with private lines, so communications would be open between the trains and stations. With five cars available, trolleys

This "summer car" on the Tangent Line of the Toledo, Fostoria & Findlay Interurban Railway allowed passengers to enjoy favorable weather. *Courtesy of the Hancock Historical Museum.*

were scheduled to leave Findlay and Fostoria at 6:00 a.m. and every hour thereafter until 11:00 p.m. The eleven o'clock train would wait for theater patrons in both cities. On Sunday afternoons and holidays, cars ran every thirty minutes. Small bags and packages traveled on the passenger coaches, while the baggage car left Findlay on the odd hours and Fostoria on the even, delivering luggage to hotels.

Although most operations went smoothly, accidents did happen. In January 1903, the *Weekly Jeffersonian* reported: "Two electric cars collided on South Main street in front of Frey's drugstore last evening. Just as the interurban car of the T. F.&F. railway was starting to back into East Sandusky street siding, car No. 8 of the city lines came along at full speed, and the two vestibules came together with a crash." No one was seriously injured, but the city car sustained substantial damage.

At the end of 1905, the driving of the "golden spike" at the intersection of Lima Street and Lima Avenue acknowledged the completion of the electric railway lines joining Pennsylvania, Ohio, Indiana and Michigan. Along the route in Hancock County were Fostoria, Arcadia, Findlay, Rawson, Mt. Cory and Bluffton.

Earlier, a representative from the *Street Railway Journal* had sent a letter to the general manager of the new line complimenting the "new enterprise" and donating a gold spike "with which to bind the final rail and tie."

The streetcars and interurbans operated successfully for many years, but on January 16, 1932, that transportation era would come to an end. "Last rites" had been held for the Toledo, Bowling Green & Southern line two years earlier, leading to the abandonment of the Western Ohio & Fostoria lines and the Findlay, Fostoria & Fremont lines.

In the October 2, 1930 *Morning Republican*, reporter W. Everett Eakin described the final passenger run between Toledo and Findlay on the Toledo, Bowling Green & Southern Traction company line with a quote from Henry Wadsworth Longfellow: "A feeling of sadness comes o'er me that my soul cannot resist." Twelve passengers traveled with Eakin on the last run of the line. "Lucky thirteen," was the conductor's comment.

Although an air of sorrow could be felt by passengers and workmen alike on this final run, they were touched by the respect shown by the hearty waving of the watchmen and trackmen as the trolley passed. Just south of Maumee, at Echo Junction, the crew separated, with some of them continuing south and the others returning to Toledo. When the northbound car sounded a long, wailing whistle, C.A. Koehl, operator of the Findlay car, obviously affected, growled, "Shut off that darn whistle!"

MAIN STREET, LOOKING NORTH, FINDLAY, OHIO   117265

Findlay streetcars ran on North Main Street. *Courtesy of the Hancock Historical Museum.*

Exploding "torpedoes," or noisemakers, on the track added a more celebratory feel to the situation.

The Toledo crew, in another show of respect and camaraderie, had whitewashed well-wishes on the final car that pulled into Findlay. Signs announcing, "Going but not forgotten," "It won't be long now," and "Rest in peace!" adorned the car.

The January 13, 1932 Findlay *Morning Republican* reported, as the final days were approaching, "The period of electric railroad transportation has thus virtually come and gone within the span of a single generation," and the advent of better roads and the popularity of automobiles caused the demise of the electric lines. "The community will bid farewell to the street cars with mixed emotions, regretting their loss much as the going of an old friend is lamented and yet realizing, of course, that change comes with the years and that it must be given the recognition to which it is entitled."

During a 2017 revitalization street project in downtown Findlay, eighty-five years after the trolleys and tracks had completed their service to the community, city workers uncovered streetcar rails. It seems that instead of ripping up the old rails when they were no longer useful, the city, over the years, had simply paved over them—multiple times.

IN THE DRIVER'S SEAT

THE GRANT MOTOR CAR COMPANY—FINDLAY

"He played to win and considered it a fluke if he didn't," writes the grandson of George Duncan Grant, the man who was instrumental in bringing an automobile manufacturing business to Findlay in 1913.

As the country embraced the newly developing automobile industry, George Grant and his brother Charles discovered that both of their Detroit-based businesses, Grant Brothers Iron Foundry and Grant Brothers Automobile Company, meshed with the making and selling of cars. The foundry produced "gray iron, brass, and aluminum castings for automobile work," according to a March 1910 article in the *Foundry*. The automobile company sold several different makes of cars, including Buick, Thomas Flyer and American Simplex.

American Simplex Motor Car Company, located in Mishawaka, Indiana, produced large luxury cars starting in 1906. At this time, Ford Motor Company in Detroit was also making expensive luxury models but elected to begin making smaller, more affordable cars, such as the Model T, around 1908. Some of the men in management at Simplex got wind of these changes and developed a car they could sell for a lower price but that would still adhere to their values of reliability. Factory manager George Salzman worked with some of his associates to create a reliable, inexpensive four-cylinder car that could be mass-produced the way the Ford Model T was being built. Salzman and his coworkers took their plans to the powers that be at Simplex, thinking their idea would be greeted enthusiastically, but no one was interested. Not to be dissuaded, Salzman began searching for other potential sources of financial backing. He had no doubts about the potential success of the car—as long as they could get adequate support.

Enter George and Charles Grant. Many of the Simplex men knew, or at least knew of, the Grant brothers of Detroit. George was the consummate car salesman, was well-respected and had favorable connections necessary to obtain the financial assistance for an upcoming company.

Charles Grant had worked for the Ford Motor Company and was manager of a Ford retail store in Detroit before he and George established the Grant Brothers Automobile Company.

In 1913, George Salzman brought several men from Mishawaka, Indiana, to Detroit with him. All were experienced in the auto industry—Salzman had been the plant manager at American Simplex, as well as an experimental engineer at E.R. Thomas Motor Company in Buffalo, New York; James Howe had been an assistant engineer at E.R. Thomas; George Waite had been a sales engineer at E.R. Thomas; and David Shaw had been treasurer for American Simplex.

The July 1913 issue of the *Automotive Trade Journal* noted:

> *Mr. Salzman has been quietly and persistently working out the problem of a thoroughly good low-priced car, this work being carried on at Mishawaka, Ind. Many severe tests and long road trips were taken over the worst roads in Indiana and Southern Michigan, and corrections and changes made until the car is now believed to be without a comeback. As soon as the Grant brothers saw this car, which Salzman drove to Detroit, they immediately set about the formation of the new company.*

So, how did the Grant Motor Car Company of Detroit wind up in Findlay, Ohio?

Although the new company had been formed in Detroit, no facility had been built or purchased to house a car manufacturer. However, they did have a temporary building for a small production run before moving. As luck would have it, Findlay Motor Company, which had been in receivership for a couple of years, was forced to close, and E.L. Ewing, the promoter, had to declare bankruptcy. On November 26, 1913, the *Detroit Free Press* reported that the Grant Motor Car Company had purchased

The Grant Motor Car Company began operations in Findlay in 1913 and was located at 400 Santee Avenue. *Courtesy of the Hancock Historical Museum.*

the Findlay Motor Company plant and would begin production within two weeks, manufacturing a roadster named the Grant. The plant, located at 400 Santee Avenue in Findlay, "is a one-story brick structure, with about 45,000 square feet of floor and is fully equipped with machinery. Its capacity is estimated at about 10,000 cars a year. Shipping facilities are said to be very favorable."

Several of the officers of the Grant Motor Car Company moved to Findlay to get the facility up and running and oversee the progress. George Grant, however, opted to remain in Detroit due to business responsibilities he had there, but he divided his time between the two cities. Fortunately for Hancock County, most of the employees working in the factory would be from Findlay and its surrounding area.

A *Republican Courier* article from November 1913 shows another view of the positive role the company would play in Findlay:

The disposal of the old Findlay Motor company plant, means much for Findlay. Thousands of dollars have been sunk in this plant, mostly Hancock county money, but now that it is in the hands of men of ability and experience, honesty and integrity, it looks as though North Findlay will experience a steady growth, and that if there are any idle men in Findlay, all can find work. Empty houses will fill up and the hum of industry will soon be rampant in that section of the city.

An article about the Grant four-cylinder roadster appeared in the *Automobile Trade Journal* in July 1913, before the company's move to Findlay. As author Len G. Shaw put it:

Some think that sensations in the automobile industry have passed, but the appearance recently on the Streets of Detroit of a natty looking little car fitted with wire wheels, bearing the name Grant, actually did cause a sensation, and when it was found that these cars are to be built in 5000 lots the first year in Detroit and will sell at the very low figure of $495 each, there was something of a stir on Automobile Row.

Production at the Findlay plant began in December 1913, following quite a bit of maintenance and renovation work on the building on Santee Avenue. With additional tasks that included removing a brick stack and renovating the area to add more floor space, relocating trucks that had been left at the plant and scrapping iron and steel casings left by the former owners, production was, not unexpectedly, fairly modest during that month; only about twenty-five cars were produced and ready to sell after the beginning of 1914. By January, the company was producing up to ten cars per day.

Each month, production numbers grew, as did the number of employees. In February 1914, for example, over one hundred employees were making fifteen cars per day, and the company was making plans to build twenty cars per day and increase the number of employees to three hundred in order to keep up with the demand for foreign and domestic orders.

One of the greatest assets of the Grant roadster was its price tag, although it still had all the bells and whistles the larger luxury models had. That is why it sold so well both in the United States and abroad. At one point, seventy-five cars were sent to Melbourne, Australia—a few every day; as soon as they had been shipped, one hundred cars were sent to London, England. Of course, the cars going to countries where people drive on the left side of the road had to be modified before being sent.

The plant had produced over 2,000 cars since its inception in Findlay. On busy days, they might make 40 cars; at slower times, perhaps 12. Between 700 and 800 cars had been shipped overseas. However, World War I had an impact on many auto companies, and Grant was no exception. For example, an order for 150 cars to be sent to England was canceled because of the war, but the company was able to ship a separate order to Australia. It was important to pack cars tightly in boxes so no parts would be loose—visualize an old typewriter enclosed in its case, only bigger…much bigger.

The rooms of the plant were laid out that so no unnecessary trips had to be made from one room to another to take parts for assembling. Up to thirty cars could be held in the assembly room at a time. If you were to travel back to August 1914 and tour the Grant Motor Car Company, here is what you might see:

First, frames are taken to the machine shop and bolted together by a modern method. In the next room, the frames are fitted with axles, engines, brakes and other parts. These elements move on to the painting room, where each part is enameled. The painting room has a drop door so paint can dry in a warm, dry area.

Then, it is time to test the frames and engines. If any flaws are found, back they go to the machine shop to be repaired.

Some Grant cars were tested by driving them from Findlay to Van Buren and back (a distance of about fourteen miles). Others traveled from the North plant on Santee Avenue to the South plant on Western Avenue. *Courtesy of the Hancock Historical Museum.*

The frames, complete with their metal parts, including engines and wheels, are transported to an assembly room by trucks. Nothing on the machine touches the floor until the tires are put on the wheels. Car bodies, on the other side of the room, are then put on the frames, adding finishing touches. After everything is put together, the car is ready for a road test. If anything is not working properly, the car is returned to the testing room to be thoroughly inspected and repaired.

By November 1914, about a year after the Grant Motor Car Company moved to Findlay, the company began to make the six-cylinder Grant Six. It was a five-passenger vehicle and, like the roadster, had all of the amenities of the more upscale cars but sold for a mere $795. It was the first six-cylinder car to sell for under $1,000.

An advertisement of the day states: "The car is built along graceful lines and presents an attractive appearance. A complete equipment, with electric starting and lighting facilities, is included in the $795 price. It is controlled by a left-hand drive, with the throttle lever under the wheel. The body is a beautiful streamline with deep and wide cushions. Transmission is in the form of a selective sliding gear, with three speeds forward, and reverse."

Grant Motor Car Company always strongly felt its competition, especially from the Ford Motor Company. Henry Ford was able to build more cars in a much more efficient manner in his plant in Detroit. With more production, he was also able to drop the price of his Model T Runabout, which competed with the Grant roadster. When Ford lowered the price of his car to $440, Grant set the price of his roadster at what he considered a "rock-bottom" price: $425.

George Grant's son, John Rands Grant, once related a story about his father and Henry Ford. Now, Grant and Ford knew each other, being in the same business. George met with Henry and told him that he (Henry) knew that George could not successfully sell his Grant car if Ford was continually lowering the price of his Model T. Ford responded, "No, no, George, we're all set. Everything is going fine. We are not going to fool around with the price of the car for some period of time. So don't give it a thought." But, according to John Grant, "Well, it wasn't but about four months later that the price of the Ford Model T went down fifty dollars."

Finally, Grant was only building the Grant Six—which sold for $795— but sales were going well. In fact, in February 1915, a second factory was to be opened to handle the assembly of Grant cars. The Table Factory on Western Avenue became an auxiliary Grant Motor Car factory. The chassis were to be built and road-tested at the Santee Avenue (North) plant, while the Western Avenue (South) plant was the venue for completing the painting and finishing work. Cars would be shipped from the Western Avenue plant.

Shipping cars across the country was no easy or inexpensive feat. In February 1915, six Grant Six cars went to Los Angeles, and four went to Omaha. The total cost for shipping the six cars via Wells Fargo Express to Los Angeles was $910, and they took four days to arrive "by fast express." From Findlay to Deshler to Chicago to Los Angeles, the ten-thousand-pound cargo was "one of the most expensive shipments which has ever left Findlay, I believe," said Albert Weitz, local Wells Fargo agent.

The acquisition of this second building added forty thousand square feet of work space, doubling the company's original capacity and allowing for the creation of thirty to forty cars per day. It was expected to be operational by March 1, after the table factory was remodeled to accommodate the automobile plant. Gem Churn factory had been located in one of the smaller buildings of the table factory and was allowed to remain.

Grant Motor Car Company employees take a break. One fellow in the back row, holding a mallet, seems to be having a bit of fun with a coworker. *Courtesy of the Hancock Historical Museum.*

Following the removal of all of the woodworking machinery from the table factory and churn factory, the plant was outfitted with automotive machinery. Since the cars would be shipped from this auxiliary plant, a large loading platform was built between the plant and the Lake Erie & Western Railroad siding. Several times a day, the chassis from the Santee plant were paraded down Main Street to the Western Avenue plant.

New Grant cars for the 1916 season included the Roadster, priced at $795, and the new Cabriolet, priced at $1,025. Both were built on Grant Six chassis, with a few alterations. The Cabriolet, a car with a top that folds down, was described in the local newspaper:

> *The new Grant Cabriolet is really a model of completeness and noticeable for its exceptionally graceful and well-balanced proportions. The body is of true Cabriolet type specially designed and developed as an enclosed car. The top may be lowered, from the windshield back, but, with the top up this new Cabriolet is strictly an enclosed body.*
>
> *The details of finish have been admirably worked out. The body is unusually roomy and is lined with gray whipcord, the upholstery being of the same fashionable material*
>
> *The windows can be lowered for ventilating and all are equipped with anti-rattle devices and the windshield is also adjustable to a variety of positions. A feature that will commend itself to all who dislike the appearance of extra tires "stuck on" the side or back of a car, is the wide storage space in the rear.*
>
> *The back opens up its full width providing unusually large storage space with ample room for storing extra tire and demountable rim in addition to luggage, repair kits, tools, etc. Like the big Grant Six touring car, the new models are finished in dark Brewster-green with black fenders, hood and running gear.*

Even though things seemed to be looking up for the new season of cars, the Grant Motor Car Company began to experience difficulty in obtaining financing in 1916. Rumors flew that the company was going to be taken over by a new corporation when a deal for financing from New York fell through. David Shaw, president and treasurer of Grant Motor Car Corporation, squelched those rumors. The company was, however, eventually able to acquire $2 million from a Chicago firm.

It turned out that the rumors were true after all. In March 1916, the Grant Motor Car Company announced news of a reorganization. A company press release stated:

Grant Motor Company of Findlay, Ohio, manufacturers of the Grant Six has been reorganized and its entire property and assets taken over by the Grant Motor Car Corporation, with a capitalization of 4,000,000. The new company absorbs all the rights and liabilities of the old company.

Andrews & Co., bankers, Chicago, together with prominent New York and Boston financial interests, have been instrumental in the formation of the new company. This large increase in capitalization means greater manufacturing facilities, and a big increase in production, the estimate for the coming year being 15,000 Grant Six automobiles.

Grant Motor Company has been engaged the last three years in the manufacture of motor cars, and during that period has become well-known throughout the country as pioneers in the manufacture of a six-cylinder car to sell for less than $1000.

The old working organization remains intact. D. A. Shaw, as president, assisted by George S. Waite, sales manager; George S. Salzman, production manager; James M. Howe, engineer, will continue as the active working heads at the plant.

Now, the question was: "Will the Grant Motor Car Company retain its factories in Findlay?" The townspeople were assured at this time that the business would remain in Findlay. Two short months later, however, the news came that the corporation had outgrown the Findlay plants and was moving everything to a new facility being built in Cleveland.

For over two and a half years, the Findlay plants of the Grant Motor Car Company had employed between two hundred and four hundred laborers. The company had been good for Findlay and Hancock County. The town remained hopeful that the plants would find new owners to take over the factories. As the *Weekly Jeffersonian* reported in May 1916, "while the removal of the Grant plant from Findlay means the loss of a big industry to Findlay, it is believed that it will have little perceptible effect on the city's condition, financially, industrially and otherwise, because of the splendid state of affairs generally prevalent in the city." The company announced that the plants would be closed in late November 1916. Later, the plant was used once again, this time as a munition factory during World War I.

Knowing that Findlay had once been the home to a car manufacturing company led one local man to research, collect, restore, parade and simply admire the Grant automobile. Bill Phillips lives in a home he built in 1992 on the same property where he was born ninety years ago. As he put it: "I came in here; I'm going out here." His home is decorated with car memorabilia in the form of books, models, plaques and photographs, as well as antique toys and other collections.

Phillips became interested in old cars when he was in high school in the 1940s, when he and a friend spied an old car at a farm on their way home from a high school athletic event in the next county. Intrigued by the odd-looking vehicle, they eventually returned to that farm and talked to the owner about purchasing the car. "He was asking eighty-five or ninety-five dollars. How would we be able to come up with that kind of money?" Phillips recalled. Somehow, they were able to raise the money and went back and bought the 1916 Franklin Touring car, hoping that "maybe we could pick up some girls!"

After high school, Bill got married, and his friend joined the army, so they ended up selling the car—for about $300. Bill recently ran it down and found that it was owned by a Franklin Car Club member. "That car would probably cost $30,000 today," he remarked.

His interest in antique cars grew, especially after he met a neighbor in the 1950s who had worked at the Grant Motor Car Company in the engine division out of Detroit. After much discussion, Phillips decided he wanted a Grant.

The first Grant he purchased and restored was a 1914 Grant roadster. He had visited the owner in Michigan, who wanted information about the Grant but had not intended to sell it. Later, though, sometime in the early 1970s, the owner sent Bill Phillips a postcard offering to sell him the car: "I don't even know if I finished reading that card before I was getting a trailer and taking my young son to Michigan to buy that '14 Grant!" He got that car up and running and eventually donated it to the Hancock Historical Museum in Findlay.

Phillips donated other cars to the museum, including a 1918 Grant Touring Coupe. Although it was not made in Findlay (the company had moved to Cleveland by then), he felt that it showed the continuation of the Grant automobile and added to the city's history.

Over the years, Phillips has gotten to know other Grant enthusiasts, corresponding with and visiting them. He visited two Grant owners in Australia and New Zealand in 2003. He helped the man in Australia get metal for his car's radiator. The Australian had found the 1914 Grant abandoned in a field and took it home to restore it. The man in New Zealand had a 1917 Grant Touring car and probably became interested in that particular line of cars because his last name was also Grant. Phillips

Grant cars were produced in Findlay from 1913 to 1916. *Courtesy of the Hancock Historical Museum.*

also corresponds with a Grant owner in Wales, as well as many owners living in the United States.

Although Bill Phillips doesn't really work on his cars much anymore, he still has a few at his home in two different garages. A yellow 1914 Grant Roadster has its original wiring and is a sight to behold.

4

KEEP ON TRUCKIN'

Adams Brothers Company—Findlay

Although they were born nearly twenty years apart and in two different states, brothers James T. and Newton M. Adams would each leave their homes at age fourteen to seek work as tinsmiths and would eventually settle in Findlay to spend their final twenty years as corporate partners, the Adams Brothers, each playing an important role in Findlay's social, business and civic arenas.

James, born in Pennsylvania in 1825, apprenticed as a tinsmith and worked in that field in Massillon, Plymouth and Findlay, Ohio, until around 1860, when he operated a hardware store for a few years. Then, he worked in the linseed oil business for eighteen years.

James's younger brother Newton traveled from his boyhood home in Plymouth, Ohio, to Corunna, Indiana, where he found work as a store clerk before enlisting in Company F, 129th Ohio Volunteer Infantry in 1863. He was a part of Sherman's March to the Sea and fought in several battles in Tennessee before returning home. After moving to Findlay in 1869, he set up shop in the tin and stove business.

James and Newton and another brother, John, formed a partnership for a foundry business in 1878—Adams Brothers Company was set up with James as president and Newton as treasurer. This company was incorporated in 1890, again with James as president.

The foundry itself was huge and housed and contained a machine shop, an office and blacksmith, boiler, molding and casting rooms. Items produced at this time included supplies for the gas and oil industry, pumps, engines and ironworks. This successful business was well known and well respected throughout northwest Ohio.

The dawn of the new century added another dimension to the company. The automotive era was upon them. In fact, the company closed a contract for building a road scraper in 1908, expecting to enlarge the factory and increase the number of workers. But it was not until after the deaths of James and Newton, in 1908 and 1909, respectively, that the next generation of Adams men would venture into the automotive industry.

The foundry was well equipped to enter this new manufacturing business. The company had been making engines for years. Machinery was already in place. Shops and other work areas could easily be adapted for additional functions.

The Adams Brothers Company on West Main Cross Street in Findlay made everything for their trucks except springs and tires. *Courtesy of the Hancock Historical Museum.*

In August 1910, the company was ready to parade its first "automobile truck, to be known as the Adams," on the streets of Findlay. Every bit of this two-ton truck—with the exception of springs and tires—was manufactured at the Adams Brothers factory.

The buyer had some flexibility in ordering an Adams. Only need the chassis? It's yours. Want something other than the Adams body? Sure! Work with the Adams designers or with one of your own. The idea was to allow the purchaser some latitude in meeting individual needs.

The two-ton Adams led the way to manufacturing other trucks. Both one- and one-and-a-half-ton trucks were being manufactured within a year.

Of course, vehicles had to be tested, not simply ridden around town. The "endurance run" of the first Adams truck traveled much of the western part of the state, from Findlay to Toledo, back to Findlay, and on to Cincinnati via Lima and Dayton. From Cincinnati back to Findlay, the truck drove through Hamilton and Columbus. Of course, in the larger cities, onlookers were treated to an examination of the novel vehicle.

The following year, a one-ton truck was loaded with sand bags weighing around 2,300 pounds and bound for Chicago. After leaving Findlay at four o'clock in the morning one Monday in August 1911, the projected time of arrival in Chicago was midnight Wednesday. Instead, the truck traveled the 250 miles with no breakdowns or other problems and arrived in Chicago at eleven o'clock Tuesday night—almost twenty-four hours earlier than expected.

The orders started rolling in, and the Adams factory on West Main Cross Street hired additional workers, increasing the workforce to 125, to fill those orders. Trucks were shipped to Springfield, Massachusetts, and Kansas City, Missouri. Other orders came from Texas and Florida. The Adams Brothers firm was now known across the nation. In time, it became known across the world, making sales to Australia and Japan.

The summer Findlay celebrated the Fort Findlay Centennial in 1912, Adams Brothers opened the factory to visitors who wanted to see how a truck was built. Guides took guests on tours of the plant, explaining the function of each machine, motor or shop. More and more orders were filled, and trucks were shipped to Los Angeles and Buffalo. Four trucks had already been sold to Findlay businesses.

The plant encompassed most of a city block and was divided into nine different departments. The foundry now contained rooms for assembling motors and chassis; a testing room; a machine shop; forging, foundry, painting and finishing departments; and woodworking and stock rooms.

In addition to offices, the two-story office building had a drafting room on the second floor, "which employs four of the best draftsmen to be found in the country."

In October 1912, the *Hancock Courier* waxed poetic regarding the new "motor fire truck" that Adams Brothers had built and "unveiled" on the streets of Findlay before sending it to its new owner in Pennsylvania. "Nothing like it was ever seen here before and all marveled at its beauty. The body of the truck is finished in fifteen coats of pure white enameled paint with gold stripes. It is thoroughly equipped with all that is required for a ladder and hose wagon and in front has a powerful searchlight. It has a 35-horse-power motor and can easily make forty miles an hour."

Finally, Findlay was ready to purchase a new fire truck from Adams Brothers. By January 1914, the truck was ready to be delivered, as the January 1, 1914 *Weekly Jeffersonian* reported. "The 60-horse-power chemical fire truck ordered by the City of Findlay will be delivered to Chief Charles Arthur Wednesday morning by Adams Brothers, who were awarded the contract to furnish the truck and equip it with a chemical cylinder, which was furnished by the department, it being removed from one of the horse-drawn wagons."

The horse-drawn wagons, however, were not being put out to pasture, so to speak. They still had their advantages, especially on muddy streets.

The Findlay Fire Department purchased an Adams firetruck in 1914. *Courtesy of the Hancock Historical Museum.*

The new truck would be primarily used in the downtown business area of Findlay, the *Weekly Jeffersonian* article went on to say, "where there is the most danger of great losses, as it can reach the scene of fire in far less time than a horse-drawn wagon."

Ten years later, in July 1924, the "new Adams fire truck" fought its last fire. Called to a barn fire on Central Avenue, the firefighters were "forced to attach the hose to the fire plug on Tiffin avenue. Quick coupling of the different sections ran the hose to the scene nearly three blocks away," according to the *Morning Republican*. But they were too late. The barn collapsed soon after the water began pelting it. Tools, hay and feed were all lost. It wasn't the fault of the "old Adams fire truck," of course; it just happened to be on its final run. The fate of the pioneer truck that had been in use for eleven years led it to the back room of the South Side station to be sold and then replaced by the American LaFrance service truck. The *Morning Republican* article continued, "After abandonment of the old service car the South Side department will have the two modern fire motor trucks and the chief's car."

Benton's Marathon Truck Stop—Williamstown

During the 1910s, automobiles and trucks had quickly caught on as an exciting yet more personal alternative to trains, which still led the way in transporting people and goods over longer distances. But, while railroad tracks covered the country from coast to coast and most points in between, car and truck traffic was limited to poorly maintained streets and roads in a more immediate area.

Around the time Adams Brothers was building trucks and the Grant Motor Car Company was building cars in Findlay, an auto enthusiast named Carl G. Fisher began peddling the idea of building a transcontinental highway from New York City to San Francisco. After all, without good roads, the car would not reach the level of importance that he foresaw. With friends in the auto industry, he was able to pledge a million dollars toward what would become the Lincoln Highway. Begun in 1913, the route was modified a few times, but the final course, which traversed thirteen states, was adopted in 1928. In Ohio, it connected East Liverpool and Van Wert, a distance of about 240 miles, much of it along already established roads. Because travelers would need to regularly add gas and oil to their vehicles and obtain food for themselves, truck stops and restaurants popped up along the new route.

The Lincoln Highway, or "old U.S. 30," cuts straight through the southern part of Hancock County. It passes Williamstown, a.k.a. "Billtown," at its intersection with Route 68, originally part of Hull's Trace. Williamstown was founded in 1834 by John W. Williams, who opened a tavern and a store there. The following year, according to R.C. Brown's *History of Hancock County*, "a State road was laid out from Bucyrus toward Fort Wayne, Ind., passing through Williamstown in its route."

The Toledo & Ohio Central (T&OC) Railroad entered this part of the county in the 1880s. "The business of the place [Williamstown] was never very great, and even the coming of the railroad did not increase it, but on the contrary, it has steadily declined, until at this time it has an appearance of forlorn lonesomeness," Dr. J.A. Kimmell wrote in his 1910 *Twentieth Century History of Findlay and Hancock County, Ohio*.

Williamstown, however, did not vanish into obscurity. By the 1950s, truck traffic was especially heavy along the Lincoln Highway, and Williamstown was about the only community in Hancock County along the route. This made it a perfect place for a truck stop and eatery.

In 1951, Findlay residents Sam and Dorothy Benton leased the building for the truck stop in Williamstown from Marathon Oil Company and successfully ran it for nearly two decades. By 1960, when they took over the operation of the attached restaurant, the business had become a family affair. Sam and Dorothy's daughter Phyllis and son John spent many of their teenage years working there.

Phyllis, four years older than John, worked in the kitchen and as a waitress beginning in junior high. A shy girl, she says it was good for her to talk to people and become more confident. Her work included anything from taking orders to washing dishes to preparing potatoes for French fries. "That was a different time," she says. They wore starched uniforms and aprons, and there were no electric dishwashers or frozen fries. Dishes were washed by hand in the kitchen sink. "Not fun," remembers Phyllis Wiegand (née Benton). French fries were homemade; peeled and cut potatoes were placed in a large jar of salt water until they were ready to fry. Many of the cooks were farm wives, and since most of them didn't drive, Phyllis added "chauffeur" to her list of responsibilities.

"Mom had never run a restaurant before," Phyllis said, "but she made it profitable, even more profitable than the trucking side." The truck stop was open twenty-four hours a day every day except Christmas. Even with two to three dozen people working a three-shift schedule, there were times Dorothy would have to fill in for a sick employee, any hour of the day or night, making the seventeen-mile drive from Findlay to Williamstown and back home again. Phyllis emphatically stated, "She worked a lot!"

Patrons of the business included locals, teenagers and, of course, truck drivers, many of whom drove for truck lines that were contracted to stop at the Williamstown service station. In fact, around fifteen truck lines held charge accounts with the stop. Truckers coming from Pennsylvania, Michigan, Indiana and Ohio hauled everything from chemicals to livestock and grain to other trucks.

When John Benton was around twelve years old, he had responsibilities at the truck stop. He would mow the yard and paint the curbs. He also collected smashed, empty oil cans that truckers had driven over, amassing three hundred at one time. In the mid-1960s, John worked on the truck service side of the business. Truckers would arrive for refueling—both their trucks and their stomachs—and John would drive their rigs to the full-service pumps to fill the tanks while the men ordered a meal. He also "washed the windshield, checked the oil and water and thumped the tires," as Don Steinman reported in an ECHO (Eagle Creek Historical Organization) newsletter. Automobiles and motorcycles received the same services. John lamented that motorcycles would often stop in ten at a time, then their riders would only purchase a gallon of gas. But John never complained about having to wash the windshield of a car with a pretty girl sitting inside.

The restaurant sold more than just meals. It also had first aid and toiletry products, jewelry, sunglasses, belts, cigarettes and pop (Ohioan for "soda"). Pop was sold in one of the four machines on the premises for ten cents a bottle—a glass redeemable bottle.

The truck stop carried diesel, premium and regular gas at three different pumps. The diesel pump had a 10,000-gallon tank, the premium pump had two 10,000-gallon tanks and the regular pump had two 6,000-gallon tanks. Sam Benton did not participate in price wars; therefore, the prices did not change over the last five years he was in business. Diesel was twenty-five cents, regular was thirty-two cents, and premium was thirty-four cents.

They also sold oil, at twenty-five to thirty cents a quart, and Cooper tires and tubes. The service attendants wore Marathon hats and blue shirts, and Sam always wore a tie.

By the late 1960s, life had changed along the Lincoln Highway. A new Route 30 became a bypass around Williamstown. Started in 1957, the road did not hinder the truck stop's sales as much as Sam had predicted. Nor did the new Interstate 75. However, the higher wages offered by several Findlay companies led to the defection of many the truck stop's workers. The truck stop simply could not compete.

After eighteen years of operation, the Bentons decided to sell the business. They had leased the building but owned the business. Phyllis described her mother's thoughts on the subject—Dorothy simply said, "I'm done!" The Bentons closed their business on October 22, 1969. Two days later, a new owner was in place, operating the concern from 7:00 a.m. to 7:00 p.m. Unfortunately, the new owner was not as successful as the Bentons had been, and the Williamstown truck stop permanently closed the following fall.

PART 5: FOOTLOOSE AND FANCY FREE—ENTERTAINMENT

1

THE SHOW MUST GO ON

Opera Houses and Theaters—Arlington, Benton Ridge, Findlay, McComb, Rawson

It may be difficult to imagine that many people in Hancock County during the late nineteenth and early twentieth centuries sought and found entertainment at their local opera houses. Granted, the buildings and fare may not have been on as grand a scale as the Sydney Opera House or Milan's La Scala, but opera houses in Benton Ridge, Rawson, Arlington and McComb offered a social and cultural venue for their patrons.

Opera houses in the small communities of Hancock County served multiple purposes. Although an opera might have been presented by a traveling troupe, these venues were just as likely to host an ice cream social, band concert or political address. They were places where locals could gather socially and be entertained or informed. Commencement exercises were often performed at the opera house. The first graduating class of 1896 in Rawson, for example, consisted of two members; their commencement was held at the Rawson Opera House, with the Findlay superintendent delivering the address.

In May 1899, Benton Ridge's Whisler Hall hosted a large assembly for a church ladies' ice cream social, where "W. H. Wittenmyer makes a good clerk to sell things for church purposes," said the *Daily Courier*. The following

Whisler Hall in Benton Ridge hosted lectures, concerts, graduations and other social and cultural events. *Courtesy of the Hancock Historical Museum.*

month, commencement exercises were held there for seven graduates who "all delivered their recitations in a very able manner," with the Benton orchestra providing music that evening.

Other types of entertainment presented at Whisler Hall in 1899 included gramophone music, a hypnosis demonstration and a military drill team, the Findlay Cadets, exhibiting their skills "of handling the implements of war."

Both Whisler Hall in Benton Ridge and the Opera House in Rawson played host to hypnotist Prof. D.S. Finton of Findlay. "His work is of the highest order, strictly moral, and highly entertaining, with none of the 'fake show' about it," remarked the Rawson superintendent of schools, A.J. Nowlan.

Several years later, more events were staged at Whisler Hall. In 1908, the Wittenmyer Cadet Band performed concerts there. As the *Republican Jeffersonian* reported, "The organization is composed of musicians of the town who have been drilled by Prof. Wittenmyer to such an extent that they can stand beside any similar organization in the county without having their glory dimmed." They traveled throughout the county, playing everything from marches to polkas to waltzes. "The band consists of twenty-four pieces, including several violins and soloists."

1897   1897

Commencement - Program,

... TO BE RENDERED ....

Saturday Evening, April 24, 1897.

Opera House, Rawson, O.

Organ Voluntary	Miss Eugenie Davis
Invocation	Rev. W. J. Green
Music—*Sunbeams*	Male Quartet
Oration—*Education Necessary to the Mainte-nance of our Government*	Cora Gorby
Oration—*Whither are we Drifting*	R. G. Myers
Music—*Goodbye Old Home*	Male Quartet
Oration—*The Model Girl*	Maud Knepper
Oration—*Honor Waits at Labor's Gate*	Morse Hartman
Music—*The Nightingale*	Trio
Oration—*Little Things*	Grace Shank
Oration—*Getting the Right Start*	Eva Wonder
Music—*Rocked in the Cradle of the Deep*	Male Quartet
Oration—*Reserved Power*	Cloys McClelland
Music—*Sunlight*	Trio
Oration—*From the Bay into the Ocean*	Maude Follabanm
Music—*Graduates Farewell*	Duet
Class Address	Rev. Albritten, D. D.
Presentation of Diplomas	Dr. L. S. Woods
Music—*Good Night*	Male Quartet
Benediction	Rev. W. J. Green

Doors Open, 7:30. Exercises Begin, 8:00—Sun Time

Admission, 25c.

This 1897 program shows the activities presented at the commencement exercises at Rawson's Opera House. *Courtesy of the Hancock Historical Museum.*

Lecturers would share their experiences with the people of Benton Ridge at Whisler Hall. In 1913, K. Bagdasarian, an Armenian student, "gave an interesting lecture in Whisler Hall on his native country and its customs." And in 1920, Reverend B.F. Miller of McClure, in Henry County, gave two lectures—one on the Philippine Islands, where he had taught for six years, and the other on the Holy Land.

Mt. Cory High School used Whisler Hall to present an evening of entertainment in 1914, with proceeds being given to benefit the Benton Ridge schools in a time of need.

Home talent (local talent) was another aspect of the opera houses. A 1921 performance of *Cuban Spy* played to a packed Whisler Hall. "It was a credit to the performers and would be an honor to a much larger village," according to the *Weekly Jeffersonian*.

In Arlington, the Crates Opera House, like many nineteenth-century opera houses, was located on the second floor of the building, with businesses below it. Plays and other entertainment were featured there, and farmers' institutes and lectures were held there.

Farmers' institutes were an important part of Hancock County's agricultural history. Many of these sessions were held in the opera houses of Benton Ridge, McComb, Arlington and Findlay. The purpose of these institutes was to educate farmers through a series of lectures. The institutes, which began in the mid-nineteenth century, grew in popularity and usefulness. By 1896–97, all eighty-eight counties of Ohio were participating. And during the winter of 1903–4, 247 institutes convened in Ohio. The institutes, sanctioned by the State Board of Agriculture and working in conjunction with Ohio State University, were held for two days and featured lectures on topics such as geology, chemistry, botany, vegetable physiology, zoology and pathology principles. These lectures would aid farmers in improving drainage methods, for example, or demonstrate animal treatments and surgical procedures a farmer might have to perform.

Newspapers of the day encouraged all farmers to attend. The institute held in Hancock County in 1882 was presented at the Opera House in Findlay. Free lectures by Ohio State University professors "are given for the benefit of all persons interested in agriculture, upon a great variety of topics in this connection. Discussions follow and much knowledge is gained from the varied experiences of the tillers of the soil."

The McComb Opera House also hosted the farmers' institute each year, but it was just as well-known for plays (featuring both professional and home talent), lectures, graduations and perhaps a bit of waywardness. Lois Pendleton, of Pendleton Lumber, shared many memories of the Opera House in McComb's 1981 sesquicentennial book. She was one of the fortunate people who experienced the Opera House in its heyday. Dramas, comedies, life lessons, good guys and bad—the Opera House offered something for everyone. Lois Pendleton related the following story in the sesquicentennial book:

> *We didn't get to attend often, so it was a real treat when we were allowed to take our hoarded dime and buy a ticket for the first row. There we shuddered*

at the crack of the bull-whip striking poor Uncle Tom, and we cried when Little Eva ascended into the scenery on her way to Heaven. We absorbed the powerful temperance lesson in "Ten Nights in a Barroom" and vowed never to touch liquor. And on a less lofty level we laughed at "Sis Perkins" and sighed with "East Lynn." We adored the shining heroes and hated the mustachioed villains. It was great!

Early in the twentieth century, McComb became what was known as a lyceum town—a place for speakers, lecturers, entertainers and musicians to provide culture from the outside world. Even lieutenant governor Warren G. Harding spoke there at a Republican rally in 1905.

In 1906, a McComb native who had moved to Cleveland to study voice, Nellie Huebbler, returned to her hometown to produce a play using hometown talent. *The Fairy Queen* did not disappoint. Each of those chosen to play a part had to provide his or her own costume, but this wasn't as difficult as it might have seemed. The girls were able to wear their white Sunday dresses, and the men wore their good suits.

Women's clothing styles of the day included large hats—hats that, if worn in the opera house, would impede the view of many patrons. A humorous tradition began when the behatted women took their seats but intentionally ignored the large sign asking that they remove their hats. The women waited for Licurgus "Old Spitz" Willoughby, a saloon owner, to stroll out onto the stage and request, in a voice larger than the sign, "Take your hats off, ladies; take your hats off." Once Old Spitz had made his announcement, the audience laughed, the women removed their hats and the show commenced.

In her reminiscences, Lois Pendleton reflected on the effects the passage of time had on the McComb Opera House. Traveling shows had been replaced by movies and radio, commencement exercises could now be held in the new high school and "Old Spitz was gone." Rumor had it that slot machines and bootleg whiskey had played a part in the building's past. Bill Shoemaker, owner of the building, saw no use for the second-floor stage of the opera house and renovated that floor into apartments.

"After his death and that of his son, his grandson disposed of the building, verifying and enlarging on the hints" and rumors, Pendleton remarked. "A still under the back stairs? A few armed bandits hastily buried under concrete? If anyone in those apartments or patrons of the downstairs room should hear a ghost, I know it will be Old Spitz saying: 'Take your hats off, ladies. Take your hats off!'"

The highly touted Marvin Opera House opened in downtown Findlay in 1893. William Marvin, a successful Findlay businessman with grand ideas, wanted to build a magnificent opera house. He traveled to various cities around the country to see what type of building he might want to emulate or, at least, to borrow some ideas. He discussed his ideas with a local architect, W.L. Kramer, and asked Kramer to draw up plans for "a structure which was determined should excel anything of the kind in the State," according to an article in the *Daily Courier*.

The *Daily Courier* labeled the Marvin Opera House, which opened on September 18, 1893, as "MR. MARVIN'S GREAT TRIUMPH." An article the following day described everything about the theater: "The building is a massive structure, 95 X 128 feet in dimensions, which does not include the lobbies, power rooms, etc. The stage is 40 by 80 feet, with a proscenium arch 30 feet high and 35 feet wide."

MARVIN THEATRE

TAKES PLEASURE IN PRESENTING

IRENE CASTLE

IN

"Dances and Fashions of 1923"

"The Best Dressed Woman In the World"

Irene Castle played the Marvin Opera House in 1922. *Courtesy of the Hancock Historical Museum.*

The venue's seating capacity was 1,500, and the "seats themselves are luxurious, and the best to be had. One can be as comfortable as though seated in their best easy chair in their own parlor. The house was filled completely with the beauty and manliness of the city."

The lights, the heating, the ventilation—nothing anywhere else could compare to what the Marvin Opera House offered. And the initial presentation, *Richard III*, was perfection itself.

William Marvin believed his role in this masterpiece was complete after years of planning and building and realizing his dream. His job was finished, and he was proud of his accomplishment. He then confidently turned over management of the opera house to his son, Willis.

Through the years, the Marvin Opera House presented dramas like *Uncle Tom's Cabin* and comedies like *Shore Acres*. High school commencements also took place there. In November 1896, something a bit more unusual occurred. Five hundred Findlay youngsters were cast in a production of the children's operetta, *Queen Flora's Day Dream* (with six speaking parts and a chorus), performing it at the Marvin Opera House.

Other entertainment centered around the sport of boxing. It was not unusual for train cars from Lima and Tiffin and Fostoria, loaded with hundreds of sports enthusiasts, to arrive at the Marvin to see a bout or two. In 1904, the *Courier Union* reported that an "enormous crowd is anticipated" to see the contest between "Biz" Mackey and Cloyce Yerger. In 1920, another fight drew an enthusiastic crowd when Kid Ryan and George Burton met. "The house was over half filled for the first of a series of boxing exhibitions to be staged by the Findlay Athletic club this winter. The crowd was enthusiastic and generously applauded the clever work of the fighters," according to a report the *Weekly Jeffersonian*.

But no one surpassed the power of "Divine Sarah." Sarah Bernhardt, the famous French actress, arrived in Findlay for a performance one evening in November 1917. She had organized her own traveling acting company in 1880 and spent many years touring Europe, Canada, the United States and South America. In her performance at the Marvin, she transformed herself into Cleopatra. As the enamored *Weekly Jeffersonian* reporter wrote:

> *The stage was in that half tone light she affected so much in the height of her career and which added so much to the idealizing of her scenes. It showed her on a couch in the center of the stage with luxurious pillows to the front, waving palms to the rear, the shadows of the back swallowing up the mere details. Supported by cushions and pillows in much the fashion*

The Marvin Opera House could seat up to 1,500 people, accommodating everything from operas and plays to silent and "talkie" films to boxing events.

of the Egyptians barge that she had used in other days, no one could have realized the handicap she now overcomes.

That "handicap" was the result of gangrene that had set into one of her legs after a fall during a performance in South America in 1905, subsequently necessitating the amputation of the limb. From that time on, she arranged parts and props so that she could perform while seated.

"Findlay is to be congratulated on having had the opportunity of seeing the great Bernhardt," the *Weekly Jeffersonian* article continued. "There was a special car that came from Lima; another was present from Fostoria; every village of the county was apparently represented in the audience."

The Fahl Brothers of Mt. Blanchard owned the Clarendon Stock Company acting troupe that played in a "tented theater" in this area during the spring and summer months—sort of an outdoor opera house. An August 1915 *Mt. Blanchard Journal* article excitedly announced the return of the company "under their own tent theatre." New plays, between-act performances, bands and orchestras were featured, and all for ten to twenty cents. "The Fahl Bros have a pleasant surprise in store for the ladies," the article promised. "Each and every lady holding a 20¢ ticket will receive a beautiful silver spoon each night."

With the advent of motion pictures, both silent and "talkies," opera houses either went the way of the dinosaur or were repurposed into movie theaters. Many continued to feature live shows, but movies were the entertainment of the future.

The Globe Theater in Arlington purchased a "new $275 picture machine" in 1916. Three years later, the theater added 140 upholstered theater chairs, elevating the floor to accommodate them. Admission to this theater ranged from six cents to twenty cents over the next several years, and the owners encouraged the entire family to come and enjoy the films. What's more, the background music for the silent films was changed twice a week.

Findlay's theaters also transitioned from live shows to moving pictures. The Majestic Theatre, built in 1905 for $30,000, opened in 1906. and featured many types of live entertainment. By 1915, however, movies had taken hold, and the season opened with films from Paramount Pictures rather than a live performance, as in years past.

In 1920, Majestic management offered a deal to youngsters who wanted to see the film *Treasure Island*. It was "milk bottle day" at the theater—the price of admission was two milk bottles. The *Weekly Jeffersonian* explained: "The

The first floor of the Majestic Theatre in Findlay could seat 540 patrons, while the balcony and gallery could each seat 460 and 500, respectively, for a total seating capacity of 1,500. *Courtesy of the Hancock Historical Museum.*

unique arrangement is under the direction of the Findlay Milk Distributors Association and the Chamber of Commerce, and is expected to result in a general cleaning up of the supply of milk bottles now resting in disuse on kitchen shelves. The 12 youngsters turning in the largest number of bottles will receive a cash prize which will be well worth the trouble of securing and scouring them."

In 1927, the Majestic became the Harris Theater. Today, it is the parking lot of Wilson's Sandwich Shop, a popular Findlay restaurant that has been in business since 1936.

The last theater to open in downtown Findlay was the State Theater, which operated from 1937 until 1976, when it was consumed by fire. Ironically, the final movie presented at the State Theater was the horror film *Burnt Offerings*.

2

A WALK IN THE PARK

REEVES PARK—ARCADIA

Entertainment such as vaudeville shows, concerts, dramatic performances, and dancing could also be found in some of the larger parks of the area. At the turn of the twentieth century, when the new electric railway line was connecting Findlay to Fostoria, promoters decided that one way to increase the number of passengers on the Toledo, Fostoria & Findlay interurban would be to create a resort that would appeal to entire families, a place with all the modern amenities: picnic grove, baseball park, tennis courts, grandstand, playgrounds and a grand pavilion for bands and orchestras to accompany those who wanted to dance.

As the interurban was being constructed, Sam Reeves, an executive with the Toledo, Fostoria & Findlay Railway and president of the Dover Canal (Ohio) Iron Works, came up with the idea of building a resort between Fostoria and Findlay and initiated its inception. The plan was set in motion, property was purchased just east of Arcadia (the halfway point between Fostoria and Findlay) and a contract was signed for the construction of a summer pavilion at a cost of $6,000. According to a June 1901 report in the *Findlay Republican*:

> *The building will be 115 feet long by eighty-two feet wide, and will be of the colonial style of architecture. There will be three stories and a deep*

basement. Around the entire building runs a twelve-foot veranda. The center of the building will be a hall with 100 X 42-foot floor space at one end of which is a stage. This may be used for dancing or for conventions. The room will be two stories high, a balcony running around the upper floor. It will be very much like the big pavilion at Cedar Point. In the basement will be a well-equipped dining room. During the season there will be amusements constantly provided, and it is not unlikely that the place will be added to some circuit.

Unfortunately, Reeves died in March 1901 at the age of thirty-one, from typhoid and heart failure, before the resort was completed. His death shocked many at work on the rail line and in the park. Reeves had been a well-respected, unassuming and philanthropic man during his lifetime. In August 1901, just before the resort was to open, officials met and decided to honor Reeves's memory by naming the resort the Sam Reeves Park.

Many acts were featured throughout that summer. "Don't miss the grand high-class vaudeville show at Sam Reeves park week of August 26th," the *Findlay Union* announced. "A long list of dramatic, comedy, acrobatic, musical and dancing artists. Round trip from either Fostoria or Findlay, including admission to the theatre, 35 cents."

During a vaudeville show in the beautiful new dance pavilion in late August 1901, a large gasoline can happened to spring a leak, drenching a pile of clothing. Someone on the veranda struck a match to light his cigar, causing the clothes to ignite. Fortunately, some quick-thinking gentlemen saw what was happening and doused the flames before they reached the gas can, averting a possible catastrophe, and the audience was none the wiser.

At first, many people were skeptical that either the railway or the park would be successful. And yet, after the first season, both had thrived. In subsequent years, many additions and improvements went into making the park even more popular. Billiard tables, bowling alleys, tennis courts, a swimming pool, a Ferris wheel, playground equipment and a café all contributed to attracting even greater crowds. And because no liquor was allowed on the premises, this family-oriented park became the place for family reunions, Sunday picnics and company events. The improved railway lines also afforded people the convenience of travel from Toledo, Fremont and Lima in addition to Fostoria, Findlay and Arcadia.

Reeves Park slowly fell into disrepair. In 1910, the Toledo, Fostoria & Findlay Railway manager offered the property to be used as a normal school for northwestern Ohio. That same year, about five hundred Apostolic Pentecostal worshipers lived at the former park. Previously, the church people had boycotted the park on the grounds that it was immoral. Now, they were holding revival meetings there, using the stage as a pulpit. The dance hall, bowling alleys and pool room became a sort of dormitory. The drink pavilion became a kitchen.

Now, because Findlay, at this time, was a "dry" town and Fostoria was "wet," people from Findlay were said to travel to Fostoria to stock up on alcoholic supplies, sometimes stopping at Reeves Park. One night, so the story goes, a besotted traveler stopped at the park revival hall and walked partway down the aisle, where the preacher apparently grabbed the inebriate and quickly anointed him with olive oil. Wiping the oil from his head, the man approached the pulpit, where an elder handed him a Bible. "An hour later a thirsty person was interviewing Fostoria barkeeps in a vain attempt to trade a Bible for a drink," reported the *Republican Jeffersonian*.

In 1913, however, the general manager of Reeves Park and the Toledo, Fostoria & Findlay announced plans to make improvements and reopen the park, though an ad in the *Hancock Courier* listed the park for sale for $10,000, highlighting the thirty-five-acre property's "beautiful grove, large pavilion and auditorium, excellent dance hall, bowling alleys and ball grounds."

The park survived for several more decades but with a different name. In 1922, the Findlay-Fostoria Amusement company took over ownership of the property and renamed it Midway Park, promising to remodel the buildings and create a more modern dance hall from the auditorium. The old dance hall would become a recreation hall for billiards and bowling.

Green Mill Gardens Dance Pavilion— Riverside Park, Findlay

Visitors to Findlay's Riverside Park in the early twentieth century marveled at the beauty of this "inland resort." Like Reeves Park, Riverside contained a dance hall and pavilion in addition to many other buildings, attractions and concessions. Also like at Reeves Park, people from around the area flocked to Riverside Park to take advantage of dances at the pavilion, theater entertainment in the auditorium, picnics in the various groves, boat rides in the artificial lakes and lounging at the bathing beach, complete with sand from Lake Erie.

The original dance hall/pavilion was built in 1907, with the lower floor of the pavilion being used as a banquet hall and the upper floor as a large dance hall. Vaudeville shows played at the 1,500-seat auditorium twice a day, and other shows were held at the House of Mirth. Other options for a day at the park during these early years might include taking the children to the playground, picnicking or eating at a café or restaurant or bowling—"alleys for both ladies and gentlemen have been especially constructed for Riverside park and its patrons." A ride on a Ferris wheel, the same one that had been at Reeves Park, might please some people, as would the merry-go-round. The more daring visitor might "Shoot the Chute." This attraction stood 75 feet above the water and had an inclined track length of 374 feet and was equipped with thirty "boats" that each held about ten people. Thrill-seekers were taken to the top of the ride by a motorized system and plunged down the chute at a rate of 136 miles per hour, ending in a misty splash into a lagoon. As safe as this sounds, a fatality did occur in 1908, when a board on a boat had loosened.

Several years later, as happens over time, the park's buildings were remodeled, enlarged or demolished.

Even after renovations, the refurbished dance hall lasted only a couple of years. By 1925, Riverside's nineteenth season, the park had been enlarged and a new $20,000 dance hall had been built. Named the "Green Mill" because a large green windmill was fastened to its roof at one time, the new pavilion drew the attention of many dancers and people-watchers. Around five hundred people attended the first dance at the official dedication of Green Mill Gardens on June 11, 1925. Dancing started at 8:00 p.m. and lasted until 11:30 p.m., with official addresses and speeches in between.

The dance pavilion had five double-door entrances, a hat and coat check room, restrooms and a shell-shaped platform for an orchestra. Lighting of the dance floor consisted of bowl-shaped lights illuminating the green and white walls. Between dances, patrons could gather in a roped-off reserved area just off the dance floor. If someone was looking for a friend from his or her hometown, signs around the floor noted areas for each neighboring community. Dances were held every night of the week except Sundays for the rest of the summer.

The lighted windmill on top of the building reached a height of seventy feet above ground and could be seen from quite a distance. By 1930, the windmill was gone, but the dance hall retained the name.

It was not only local bands and orchestras that played at the Green Mill. In 1927, Phil Baxter and his Texas Tommies, from Dallas, played their

Green Mill Gardens at Riverside Park in Findlay hosted famous musical acts and held dances for several decades. *Courtesy of the Hancock Historical Museum.*

unique style of syncopated jazz there. The *Morning Republican* reported: "The orchestra is of 10 pieces and is recognized as one of the leading dance bands of the country. Phil Baxter, himself, is of the nation's greatest jazz pianists." Over the years, other famous bands and their leaders came to Findlay: the Glenn Miller Band, the Count Basie Band, Guy Lombardo, Ozzie Nelson, Stan Kenton, the Dorseys, Woody Herman.

The big bands faded, and rock and roll emerged. Also, roller skating had become as popular as dancing at the Green Mill, although the dance floor took a beating. The 1960s saw more local bands playing at the Green Mill and other local venues. An advertisement in a July 1969 *Republican Courier* announced a "Pop Fest" at Green Mill Gardens featuring six live bands: Naked Onion, Mixed Emotions, Heel & Soul, Organized Confusion, The Other Half and One More. Dance contest winners and "battle of the bands" winners "will appear on the LIVELY SPOT SHOW, CKLW-TV." The festival was sponsored by the Humane Society, and the ad noted that security guards would be present.

After over fifty years as an entertainment mecca, Green Mill Gardens was going the way of other older structures. A panel recommended to city council in September 1977 that the building that had been used as a venue to entertain dancers and roller skaters for decades be torn down. The structure had deteriorated over the years and was not only unsafe but was causing

Today, near where the Green Mill Gardens once stood, visitors can enjoy concerts in Riverside Park at the Allen P. Dudley Memorial Band Shell. *Courtesy of the author.*

erosion to the banks of the Blanchard River. In December 1977, one Findlay resident urged city council not to raze Green Mill until possible investors, interested in restoring and operating the site, could be found. However, in February 1978, Green Mill Gardens was razed. The commission stated that the building would be replaced by something else that was needed, possibly parking space. Today, it is indeed an expanded parking area-not far from the Allen P. Dudley Memorial Band Shell, where visitors to Riverside Park can still enjoy music.

SELECTED BIBLIOGRAPHY

Bauman, Pat, Rosalinda Paul and Renee Smith. *Back to Sandusky Street*. Findlay, OH: Allegra Print & Imaging, 2009.

Beardsley, D.B. *History of Hancock County*. Springfield, OH: Republic Printing Company, 1881.

Bordman, Georgiana N. *Odd Operas for Eventide*. Boston: Walter H. Baker & Co., 1893.

Brown, Robert C. *History of Hancock County, Ohio*. Chicago: Warner, Beers & Co., 1886.

Centennial Biographical History of Hancock County, Ohio. New York: Lewis Publishing Co., 1903.

Herstory: Voices from the Past. Findlay, OH: Hancock Historical Museum, 1996.

Kimmell, Dr. J.A. *Twentieth Century History of Findlay and Hancock County, Ohio*. Chicago: Richmond-Arnold Publishing Co., 1910.

Mollenkopf, Jim. *The Great Black Swamp*. Toledo, OH: Lake of the Cat Publishing, 1991.

Mt. Blanchard Sesquicentennial: 1830–1980. Mt. Blanchard (Ohio) Historical Society, 1980.

Rawson Sesquicentennial. 2005.

Smith, Don E. *Findlay's Pattern Glass*. Fostoria, OH: Gray Printing Company, 1970.

Spaeth, Esther, and Joyce Rossman. *Jenera's 100th*. Findlay, OH: Millstream Press, 1983.

Steinman, Don, ed. *The ECHO.* Mt. Blanchard, OH.

The Village of Arlington, 1834–1984. Arlington Senior Citizens, 1984.

PERIODICALS

Arlingtonian (Arlington, OH)

Collier's Magazine

Courier Union (Findlay, OH)

Daily Courier (Findlay, OH)

Findlay (OH) Courier

Findlay (OH) Daily Jeffersonian

Findlay (OH) Jeffersonian

Findlay (OH) Republican

Findlay (OH) Republican Courier

Findlay (OH) Union

Findlay (OH) Weekly Republican

Hancock County (OH) Herald

Hancock (OH) Courier

McComb (OH) Herald

Morning Republican (Findlay, OH)

Mt. Blanchard (OH) Journal

Republican Jeffersonian (Findlay, OH)

Times (Chicago, IL)

Weekly Jeffersonian (Findlay, OH)

USEFUL WEBSITES

Chronicling America. chroniclingamerica.loc.gov.

Community Archive Findlay-Hancock County Public Library. findlaylibrary.advantage-preservation.com.

Find A Grave. findagrave.com.

Findlay Courier. thecourier.com.

Free Family History and Genealogy Records. familysearch.org.

Google Books. books.google.com.

Library of Congress. loc.gov.

National Chicken Council. nationalchickencouncil.org.
Newspaper Archive. newspaperarchive.com.
Ohio History Connection. ohiohistory.org.
Sanborn Fire Maps Collection. loc.gov/collections/sanborn-maps.

INDEX

S

Shawtown 103, 104, 106, 134, 135
State Theater 174
streetcars 12, 138, 139, 140, 141,
     142

T

tile factory 57, 58, 59, 60, 62, 64
Toledo, Fostoria & Findlay (TF&F)
       Electric Railway 140, 141
Treece Peerless Beef Hoist 69
trolley 140, 141

U

Union Township 103

V

Van Buren 20, 38, 58, 135

W

Washington Township 57, 103
Waterloo Mill 21, 23
Whisler Hall 165, 166, 167, 168
Williamstown 105, 158, 159, 160,
     161

ABOUT THE AUTHOR

Teresa Straley Lambert holds a bachelor's degree in elementary education and secondary social studies and a master's degree in gifted education from Bowling Green State University. She taught and worked with academically gifted students for nearly thirty years.

Following her retirement from teaching, she melded her interests of history, cemeteries, travel and photography to create *The ABCs of Gravestone Symbols*, an alphabet book she wrote in verse and illustrated with photographs she shot during visits to hundreds of cemeteries throughout the United States and Europe, suggesting symbology for images carved on tombstones. She has published stories, poems and articles in various educational journals, children's magazines and newspapers. Her photos can be viewed at her website Photos & More (lambertphotosandmore.vpweb.com), Fine Art America (fineartamerica.com/profiles/teresa-lambert.html) or her Facebook page: "Dead Ends – Teresa Straley Lambert."

Teresa and her husband, Randy, reside in Findlay, Ohio, and enjoy traveling the country in their VW camper or flying off to fascinating destinations. Quite often, cemeteries are involved.

Visit us at
www.historypress.com